Open Knowledge Base and Question Answering Workshop (OKBQA 2016)

Held at the 26th International Conference on Computational Linguistics (COLING 2016)

Osaka, Japan
11 December 2016

ISBN: 978-1-5108-3324-1

Preface

The Workshop on Open Knowledge Base and Question Answering Workshop (OKBQA 2016) took place in Osaka on 11 December 2016, as part of COLING 2016. The huge and rapidly increasing amount of structured and unstructured data available on the Web makes it both possible and necessary to support users in finding relevant information. The trend moves more and more towards smart knowledge services that are able to find information, aggregate them, draw inferences, and present succinct answers without requiring the user to wade through a large number of documents. The novel avenues made possible by knowledge services are numerous and diverse, including ubiquitous information access (from smartphones, tablets, smart watches, etc.), barrier-free access to data (especially for the blind and disabled) and knowledge discovery.

Over the last years, several challenges and calls for research projects have pointed out the dire need for pushing natural language interfaces. In this context, the importance of Semantic Web data as a premier knowledge source is rapidly increasing. But we are still far from having accurate natural language interfaces that allow handling complex information needs in a user-centric and highly performant manner. The development of such interfaces requires the collaboration of a range of different fields, including natural language processing, information extraction, knowledge base construction and population, reasoning, and question answering.

The main goal of this workshop is to join forces in the collaborative development of open frameworks for knowledge extraction and question answering, to share standards, and to foster the creation of an ecosystem of tools and benchmarks.

The call for papers for OKBQA 2016 was issued in September 2016 and elicited a good number of high-quality submissions, each of which was peer-reviewed by three members of the programme committee. At the end we accepted six submissions as long papers, and ten as short papers. Our technical programme combined five oral long papers, two oral short papers and seven poster papers.

We would like to thank all the people who have contributed to the organization and delivery of this workshop: the authors who submitted such high quality papers; the programme committee for their high quality, prompt and thoughtful reviewing; the keynote speakers; the COLING 2016 organizing committees, the workshops chairs, the participants in the workshop; and future readers of these proceedings for your shared interest in this exciting new area of research. Finally, we most gratefully acknowledge the support of our sponsor: Korea Advanced Institute of Science and Technology (KAIST), Semantic Web Research Center (SWRC), KAIST School of Computing, Institute for Information & communications Technology Promotion (IITP) and National Research Foundation of Korea (NRF).

Welcome to OKBQA 2016,
OKBQA organizers

Organisers

Key-Sun Choi, KAIST, Korea

Christina Unger, Universität Bielefeld, Germany

Piek Vossen, Vrije Universiteit Amsterdam, Netherlands

Jin-Dong Kim, Database Center for Life Science (DBCLS), Japan

Axel-Cyrille Ngonga Ngomo, Universität Leipzig, Germany

Teruko Mitamura, Carnegie Mellon University, USA

Programme Committee

Anastasia Krithara, Institute of Informatics and Telecommunications (IIT), Greece

André Freitas, University of Passau, Germany

Ashutosh Jadhav, IBM, USA

Axel-Cyrille Ngonga Ngomo, University of Leipzig, Germany

Christina Unger, Universität Bielefeld, Germany

Eun-kyung Kim, KAIST, Korea

Filip Ilievski, VU University Amsterdam, Netherlands

Frank Schilder, Thomson Reuters, USA

Giorgos Giannopoulos, Athena Research Center, Greece

Gosse Bouma, University of Groningen, Netherlands

Hady Elsahar, Laboratoire Hubert Curien, France

Jin-Dong Kim, Database Center for Life Science (DBCLS), Japan

Key-Sun Choi, KAIST, Korea

Marco Rospocher, FBK, Italy

Marieke van Erp, Vrije Universiteit Amsterdam, Netherlands

Michel Dumontier, Stanford University, USA

Piek Vossen, Vrije Universiteit Amsterdam, Netherlands

Pum-mo Ryu, Busan University of Foreign Studies, Korea

Ricardo Usbeck, University of Leipzig, Germany

Roberto García, Universitat de Lleida (UdL), Spain

Sadao Kurohashi, Kyoto University, Japan

Stefano Borgo, Laboratory for Applied Ontology, Italy

Teruko Mitamura, Carnegie Mellon University, USA

Vanessa Lopez, IBM, USA

Invited Keynote Speakers

Sebastian Riedel, University College London (UCL)

Noriko Kando, National Institute of Informatics (NII)

Feature Talkers

Jin-Dong Kim, Database Center for Life Science (DBCLS)

Table of Contents

Conference Program

Sunday, December 11, 2016

9:00–9:10   *Opening*

9:10–10:00   *Keynote by Sebastian Riedel, "Inferbeddings: Reading, Reasoning and Programming with Vector Representations"*

10:00–10:20   *Featured Talk by Jin-Dong Kim, "Introduction to OKBQA framework: toward an open community collaboration for QA pipelines"*

10:20–10:50   *Break*

Session oral 1

10:50–11:20   *Using Wikipedia and Semantic Resources to Find Answer Types and Appropriate Answer Candidate Sets in Question Answering*
Po-Chun Chen, Meng-Jie Zhuang and Chuan-Jie Lin

11:20–11:50   *Large-Scale Acquisition of Commonsense Knowledge via a Quiz Game on a Dialogue System*
Naoki Otani, Daisuke Kawahara, Sadao Kurohashi, Nobuhiro Kaji and Manabu Sassano

11:50–12:00   *Poster Lightning Talks*

12:00–14:00   *Lunch (Setting of the poster)*

14:00–14:45   *Keynote by Noriko Kando*

Session oral 2

14:45–15:05 *A Hierarchical Neural Network for Information Extraction of Product Attribute and Condition Sentences*
Yukinori Homma, Kugatsu Sadamitsu, Kyosuke Nishida, Ryuichiro Higashinaka, Hisako Asano and Yoshihiro Matsuo

15:05–15:25 *Combining Lexical and Semantic-based Features for Answer Sentence Selection*
Jing Shi, Jiaming Xu, Yiqun Yao, Suncong Zheng and Bo Xu

15:25–16:00 *Break, Poster session*

Session poster

15:25–16:00 *An Entity-Based approach to Answering Recurrent and Non-Recurrent Questions with Past Answers*
Anietie Andy, Mugizi Rwebangira and Satoshi Sekine

15:25–16:00 *Answer Presentation in Question Answering over Linked Data using Typed Dependency Subtree Patterns*
Rivindu Perera and Parma Nand

15:25–16:00 *BioMedLAT Corpus: Annotation of the Lexical Answer Type for Biomedical Questions*
Mariana Neves and Milena Kraus

15:25–16:00 *Double Topic Shifts in Open Domain Conversations: Natural Language Interface for a Wikipedia-based Robot Application*
Kristiina Jokinen and Graham Wilcock

15:25–16:00 *Filling a Knowledge Graph with a Crowd*
GyuHyeon Choi, Sangha Nam, Dongho Choi and KEY-SUN CHOI

15:25–16:00 *Pairing Wikipedia Articles Across Languages*
Marcus Klang and Pierre Nugues

15:25–16:00 *SRDF: Extracting Lexical Knowledge Graph for Preserving Sentence Meaning*
Sangha Nam, GyuHyeon Choi, Younggyun Hahm and KEY-SUN CHOI

Session oral 3

17:00–17:10   *Closing*

Using Wikipedia and Semantic Resources to Find Answer Types and Appropriate Answer Candidate Sets in Question Answering

Po-Chun Chen, Meng-Jie Zhuang, and Chuan-Jie Lin
Department of Computer Science and Engineering
National Taiwan Ocean University
No 2, Pei-Ning Road, Keelung, Taiwan ROC
`{pcchen.cse, mjzhunag.cse, cjlin}@ntou.edu.tw`

Abstract

This paper proposes a new idea that uses Wikipedia categories as answer types and defines candidate sets inside Wikipedia. The focus of a given question is searched in the hierarchy of Wikipedia main pages. Our searching strategy combines head-noun matching and synonym matching provided in semantic resources. The set of answer candidates is determined by the entry hierarchy in Wikipedia and the hyponymy hierarchy in WordNet. The experimental results show that the approach can find candidate sets in a smaller size but achieve better performance especially for ARTIFACT and ORGANIZATION types, where the performance is better than state-of-the-art Chinese factoid QA systems.

1 Introduction

1.1 Motivation

Answer type is the semantic category of an expected answer to a given question. Typical QA systems use different strategies to deal with different answer types (Allam and Haggag, 2012). If an answer type is a named entity type such as PERSON or LOCATION, a named entity recognition system (NER) is usually used to identify person names or location names as answer candidates.

NER has been a success for PERSON and LOCATION types (Nadeau and Sekine, 2007), but not for other NE types, especially ARTIFACT such as movies or songs. There are too many ARTIFACT types and most of them are difficult to be automatically recognized.

This paper proposed an alternative way to decide the answer type and the set of answer candidates at the same time. An answer type can be a Wikipedia category or a term in WorNet. Answer candidates are Wikipedia entry titles. By doing so, question answering can be no longer restricted by the ability of NER systems. The set of answer candidates can also be up-to-date since Wikipedia is frequently maintained. Although this study was done on Chinese datasets, our methods are mostly automatic and it is not hard to find comparable semantic resources in different languages. Adapting our methods to another language is possible.

1.2 Related Work

Question answering (QA) has been studied since 1990s. Large-scale benchmarks developed by international evaluation projects improved the performance of QA techniques in a great deal. Since 1999, TREC (**T**ext **RE**treival Conference) has held QA tracks for several times dealing with English monolingual question answering (Dang *et al.*, 2007). NTCIR (**NII T**estbeds and **C**ommunity for **I**nformation access **R**esearch) dealt with multilingual QA in Japanese and Chinese (Sasaki *et al.*, 2007), while CLEF supported multilingual QA in European languages (Peñas *et al.*, 2014).

Proceedings of the Open Knowledge Base and Question Answering (OKBQA) Workshop,
pages 1–10, Osaka, Japan, December 11 2016.

Two benchmarks on Chinese QA have been developed in NTCIR-5 CLQA1 (Sasaki *et al.*, 2005) and NTCIR-6 CLQA2 tracks (Sasaki *et al.*, 2007). Totally 350 Chinese questions with answers have been created. They are all factoid questions. Complex questions were studied in NTCIR-7 and NTCIR-8 (Sakai *et al.*, 2010).

Most QA systems predefined several answer types and used different approaches to identify candidates of answers. Some used semantic resources (Harabagiu *et al.*, 2006; Moldovan *et al.* 2007) and others used named entity recognition (NER) systems (Lee *et al.* 2007; Kwok *et al.* 2007; Lee *et al.*, 2008; Sacaleanu *et al.*, 2008). The ability of NER systems will affect the performance of QA systems.

Wikipedia-based QA is also a hot topic. Most research groups treated Wikipedia as a knowledge base (Furbach *et al.*, 2008; Waltinger *et al.*, 2008). They analyzed sentences in Wikipedia articles to find answers. Buscaldi and Rosso (2006) mapped common answer types to top-level Wikipedia categories in order to verify answers. Their method uses coarse-grained answer types, while ours focuses on fine-grained answer types. The closest research to our work was done by Adafre and van Genabith (2008), but they treated the substring matching between Wikipedia categories and answer types in WordNet as a scoring feature. They did not use the whole hierarchy of WordNet nor Wikipedia, either.

This paper is organized as follows. Section 2 describes the proposed approach to determine answer types by Wikipedia and semantic resources. Section 3 explains how to determine answer candidate sets. Section 4 discusses the experimental results and Section 5 concludes this paper.

2   Answer Type Determination

Answer type is the semantic category of the information that a question is asking for. It is usually the semantic category of the sense described in a question focus.

Question focus of a question is the longest noun phrase (NP) which describes the expected answer. It can be the interrogative noun phrase (WHNP) without the interrogative word, such as "日本城市" (*Japanese city*) in the question "二次世界大戰時[哪個日本城市]遭投原子彈" ([*Which Japanese city*] *was atomic-bombed during World War II*, where the WHNP is bracketed and the question focus is underlined). It can also be the complement NP of a copula in a question, such as "一九九九年時國際足協主席" (*the president of FIFA in 1999*) in the question "誰是一九九九年時國際足協主席" (*Who was the president of FIFA in 1999*).

Wikipedia is a collaborative encyclopedia contributed by real users around the world. Each Wikipedia entry is often classified into several categories by its authors. These categories are also user-created, so are the hierarchical relationships between the categories. Here is an example of the semantic hierarchy where the Chinese Wikipedia entry "微軟" (Microsoft) belongs to:

Entry: 微軟 (Microsoft)
　→ Category: 微軟 (Microsoft)
　　→ Category: 美國軟體公司 (Software companies of the United States)
　　　→ Category: 各國軟體公司 (Software companies by country)
　　　　→ Category: 軟體公司 (Software companies)
　　　　　→ Category: 科技公司 (Technology companies)
　　　　　　→ Category: 各行業公司 (Companies by industry)
　　　　　　　→ Category: 各類公司 (Companies by type)
　　　　　　　　→ Category: 各類組織 (Organizations by activity)
　　　　　　　　　→ Category: 組織 (Organizations)
　　　　　　　　　　→ Category: 社會 (Society)
　　　　　　　　　　　→ Category: 頁面分類 (Fundamental categories)

As we can see, if we know the answer type of a given question is "軟體公司" (software company), all Wikipedia entries under that category, such as "微軟" (Microsoft), are appropriate answer candidates. We will discuss different methods to extract the longest Wikipedia category title from a given question focus in the following subsections.

2.1 Maximum Matching Strategy

The first straightforward method to extract an answer type from a question focus is to identify a Wikipedia category title by maximum matching algorithm. But because all these strings are noun phrases, the matched substring must also be a meaningful head of the question focus. This can be ensured by syntactic structure (such as removing of prepositional phrases) or trailing-matching strategy (i.e. matching the longest trailing substring). This kind of expected answer type will be referred to as **Wikipedia-category answer type** (WKtype) throughout this paper. Two examples are given as follows.

> Q1: 一九九九年時聯合國秘書長是誰？
> (Who was Secretary-General of the United Nations in 1999?)
> QFocus: 一九九九年時聯合國秘書長 (United Nations Secretary-General in 1999)
> WKtype: 聯合國秘書長 (United Nations Secretary-General)
>
> Q2: 微軟公司推出的辦公室套裝軟體叫什麼？
> (What is the name of the office software suite produced by Microsoft?)
> QFocus: 微軟公司推出的辦公室套裝軟體 (the office software suite produced by Microsoft)
> WKtype: 軟體 (software)

In both examples, the matched Wikipedia category titles ("聯合國秘書長" and "軟體") are trailing substrings of the question foci (denoted by QFocus). Sometimes the question focus itself is a Wikipedia category title.

As a backing method, we also define the maximum matching of a WordNet term in a question focus to be its **WordNet-term answer type** (WNtype). We use an extension version to develop our QA system, which was the Traditional Chinese version WordNet[1] extended by adding synonyms collected in the Extended Version of Tongyici Cilin[2] (同義詞詞林擴展版), a thesaurus collecting large sets of Chinese synonyms. In the two examples above, their WordNet-term answer types and their Wikipedia-category answer types happen to be the same.

2.2 Synonym Substitution and Maximum Matching

An important issue of maximum matching is the paraphrase problem. The maximum matching might fail to catch the longest one if a question focus is written in an expression different from a synonymous Wikipedia category title.

To solve such a problem, we proposed two different methods to substitute synonyms in a question focus and perform maximum matching as usual. The two methods used different semantic resources explained as follows. Sales *et al.* (2016) dealt with this problem by decomposing a category name into core+modifiers and measuring the similarity with word2vector (Mikolov *et al.*, 2013). It is possible to adopt their methods in the future.

Tongyici Cilin synonym substitution
First, all Tongyici Cilin terms in the question focus are identified. By substituting these Cilin terms with their synonyms, a lot of new QFocus strings can be enumerated. The longest Wikipedia category title that can be matched in these new QFocus strings is the final decision, which we will refer to as the **Cilin-rephrased Wikipedia-category answer type** (CKtype) throughout this paper. For example,

> Q3: 哪家是一九九八年最大的行動電話製造商？
> (What was the biggest mobile phone manufacturer in 1998?)
> QFocus: 行動電話製造商 (mobile phone manufacturer)
> ↓ 行動電話 = 手提電話 *in Tongyici Cilin*
> CKtype: 手提電話製造商 (mobile phone manufacturers)
> WKtype: N/A

---

[1] http://cwn.ling.sinica.edu.tw/ *and* http://lope.linguistics.ntu.edu.tw/cwn/
[2] http://ir.hit.edu.cn/ *and* http://www.ltp-cloud.com/

In this example, its WKtype cannot be determined because no matching of Wikipedia categories can be found. But by substituting "行動電話" (mobile phone) with its synonym "手提電話" (mobile phone) in Tongyici Cilin, the new QFocus string "手提電話製造商" (mobile phone manufacturers) itself is a Wikipedia category title and becomes the CKtype of this question.

The reason of using Tongyici Cilin instead of Chinese WordNet is that Cilin contains larger sets of synonyms in a sufficient number.

Wikipedia synonym substitution
It is okay to apply the method introduced in the previous subsubsection with a different resource of synonyms if available. In this paper, we try to recognize synonyms in Wikipedia so that we can handle named entities in a greater extent. The detected answer type will be referred to as the ***Wikipedia-rephrased Wikipedia-category answer type*** (KKtype) throughout this paper

Wikipedia does not have features denoting synonyms. The closest one is "重定向至" (redirect) page. A redirect page states that the information of an expression e_1 is contained in another Wikipedia entry e_2, mostly because e_1 is an alternative expression of e_2. For example, both "太空船" (spaceship) and "太空飛行器" (spaceplane) are redirected to the Wikipedia entry "太空載具" (spacecraft). We treat these terms connected by the redirect relationship as one type of ***Wikipedia synonyms***. (More Wikipedia synonym types will be introduced in Section 3.1.) The following example shows how to find an answer type by substituting Wikipedia synonyms.

> Q4: 一九九九年時國際足協主席是誰？
> (Who was the president of FIFA in 1999?)
> QFocus: 國際足協主席 (president of FIFA)
> ↓ 國際足協 = 國際足球聯合會 in Wikipedia
> CKtype: 國際足球聯合會主席 (presidents of FIFA)
> WKtype: 主席 (president)

In this example, its WKtype is "主席" (president). But after substituting "國際足協" (FIFA) with its Wikipedia synonym "國際足球聯合會" (FIFA), a more specific Wikipedia category title "國際足球聯合會主席" (presidents of FIFA) can be matched and becomes the KKtype of this question.

WordNet maximum matching after synonym substitution
Again as a backing, we can perform maximum matching of WordNet terms in CKtype and KKtype if available. The matched term will be referred to as the ***Cilin-rephrased WordNet-term answer type*** (CNtype) and the ***Wikipedia-rephrased WordNet-term answer type*** (KNtype) throughout this paper. Note that CNtype and KNtype may be different from WNtype, if the synonym substitution happens at the head of the question focus. The following example demonstrates how KNtype is determined.

> Q5: 請問涉嫌對台軍售弊案的前法國外長為誰？
> (Which former French Minister of Foreign Affairs was involved in the Taiwan's armament purchase scandal?)
> QFocus: 前法國外長 (former French Minister of Foreign Affairs)
> ↓ 外長 = 外交部長 in Wikipedia
> KKtype: 法國外交部長 (French Foreign Ministers)
> KNtype: 部長 (Ministers)
> WNtype: 外長 (Foreign Ministers)

In this example, its WNtype is "外長" (foreign minister) matched in the original question focus. But after substituting "外長" with its Wikipedia synonym "外交部長" (foreign minister) and extracting the KKtype "法國外交部長" (French foreign ministers), its head "部長" (minister) becomes its KNtype. The term "外長" is an infrequent abbreviation of "外交部長".

3 Answer Candidate Set Determination

3.1 Entries under a Specific Wikipedia Category

Among all the answer types introduced in Section 2, WKtype, CKtype, and KKtype are Wikipedia category titles. All the Wikipedia entries in these categories and their sub-categories are answer candidates. We will refer to such kind of answer candidate sets as ***Wikipedia-entry candidates*** (WKcand).

Note that an answer candidate from Wikipedia will be further extended with its Wikipedia synonyms in order to increase the probability of matching in the knowledge base of a QA system. Besides redirect relationships, we also derive synonymous terms by removing specific punctuations or phrases. All the Wikipedia synonym cases are listed in Table 1 with examples.

Synonym Case	Origin Term	Synonym
Redirect pages	"太空船" (spaceship)	"太空載具" (spacecraft)
Disambiguation pages	"豐田汽車" (Toyota Motor Corporation)	"豐田" (Toyota) *which has a disambiguation saying that "豐田汽車" is one of its possible meanings*
Disambiguation tags	"Trainspotting (film)"	"Trainspotting" *where the disambiguation tag "(film)" is removed; the tag denotes that the entry is about a film*
Comma-separated clauses	"Bothell, Washington"	"Bothell" *where the complement phrase is removed*
Interpuncts	"哈利·波特" (Harry Potter)	"哈利波特" (Harry Potter) *where "·", an interpunct inserted between first name and last name is removed*

Table 1. Cases of Wikipedia Synonyms

3.2 WordNet-Connected Wikipedia Entries

The answer types WNtype, CNtype, and KNtype are WordNet terms. We proposed two methods to bridge between Wikipedia and WordNet in order to obtain an up-to-date answer candidate set which are modern proper nouns in the following subsubsections.

There are two reasons that we need to bridge these two resources. (1) We do not use the set of hyponyms in WordNet directly, because WordNet terms are often common words rather than proper nouns. (2) The hierarchy of Wikipedia categories does not always stick to hypernym relationship. For example, one of the categories of the entry "台北市市長" (Mayor of Taipei) is "台北市政府" (Government of Taipei), which is not hypernymy but rather ontological relationship. Ponzetto and Strube (2007) have made a study on the hierarchy of Wikipedia. We would try to distinguish IS-A relationships from ontological relationships in the future.

Selecting entries under Wikipedia categories having heads of WordNet answer types
During the development of our QA system, each Wikipedia category was assigned a "WordNet head" which was the longest trailing substring of its title being a WordNet term. After a WordNet answer type is determined, its answer candidates are those Wikipedia entry titles which belong to any category having a WordNet head as a synonym or hyponym of the WordNet answer type. We will refer to such kind of answer candidate sets as ***WordNet-connected Wikipedia-category candidates*** (NCcand). For example,

Q6: 請問美國史上最大宗的企業破產事件為哪一家企業?
  (What is largest company bankruptcy case in the US history?)
WNtype: 企業 (enterprise)
Answer: 安隆公司 (Enron)
  → Category: 美國已結業公司 (Defunct companies of the United States)
    ↳ Head: 公司 (company) *in the WordNet synset* {企業, 公司, 事業} (enterprise)

The question's WNtype is "企業" (enterprise). Its correct answer "安隆公司" (Enron) belongs to a Wikipedia category "美國已結業公司" (Defunct companies of the United States). The category's WordNet head is "公司" (company), which is a synonym of "企業" (enterprise) in WordNet. So the correct answer is successfully included in the answer candidate set by this method.

Selecting entries whose titles have heads of WordNet answer types
The second method to bridge between Wikipedia and WordNet is to match the longest WordNet term in a Wikipedia entry title itself. We call it the "WordNet head" of a Wikipedia entry. A Wikipedia entry is an answer candidate if its WordNet head is a synonym or hyponym of WNtype. We will refer to such kind of answer candidate sets as ***WordNet-connected Wikipedia-entry candidates*** (NEcand).

In the previous example, the correct answer "安隆公司" (Enron) has a WordNet head "公司" (company), which is a synonym of the WNtype "企業" (enterprise). So the correct answer is also successfully included in the answer candidate set by this method.

4   Experiments

4.1   Experiment Setup

Our main interest in this study is to detect a precise answer type and determine its answer candidate set when NER has its limitation, especially for the classes of artifacts and organizations. Unfortunately there are not many QA benchmarks providing answer type information, nor providing evaluation results according to individual answer types. Hence we chose NTCIR QA datasets even if the number of questions were not large enough.

Two benchmarks on Chinese QA have been developed in NTCIR (Sasaki et al., 2005; Sasaki et al., 2007). NTCIR-5 CLQA1 constructed 200 questions and NTCIR-6 CLQA2 tracks constructed 150 questions classified in nine coarse-grained answer types. We only focused on 4 types including PERSON, LOCATION, and especially ARTIFACT and ORGANIZATION, because they were harder to be answered correctly in the previous evaluation.

Top 1000 relevant documents for each question were retrieved by a typical tf.idf VSM IR module from the official NTCIR CLQA corpus. Answer candidates were searched inside these relevant documents and ranked by several scoring functions in our previous QA system (Lin and Liu, 2008) which included frequencies of candidates and keywords, and their distances in a document.

The usefulness of answer type determination methods is measured in terms of the size of the answer candidate set and its coverage of correct answers. The performance of a QA system is evaluated by MRR (mean reciprocal rank, the average of the inverse of the highest rank where a correct answer is proposed) and Top-1 accuracy (the percentage of questions whose top-1 answers are correct).

4.2   Performance Upper Bound

Table 2 depicts upper bound of our system. There are totally 247 questions in ARTIFACT (ART), ORGANIZATION (ORG), LOCATION (LOC), and PERSON (PRS) types. Among them, only 221 questions have explicit question foci. The other questions are expressed only by interrogative words.

Among these 221 questions, the correct answers of 196 questions are Wikipedia entry titles. But for only 177 of them, the correct answers appear in their top 1000 relevant documents, so the upper bound performance of the baseline QA system is 0.792.

# \ Atype	ART	ORG	LOC	PRS	All
Q with Focus	20	31	57	113	221
QFocus with Wiki Ans	15	29	56	96	196
QFocus with Wiki Ans in 1000doc	15	27	53	80	175

Table 2. Number of Questions in Four Answer Types

4.3   Coverage of Correct Answers in Answer Candidate Sets

Several answer candidate sets were generated by using 4 answer-type determination methods and 3 candidate-set extraction methods. Their definitions are:

- WKtype: the maximum matched Wikipedia category title in a question focus
- CKtype: the maximum matched Wikipedia category title in a Cilin-rephrased question focus
- KKtype: the maximum matched Wikipedia category in a Wikipedia-rephrased question focus
- KNtype: the maximum matched WordNet term in a Wikipedia-rephrased question focus
- WKcand: all entries under a Wikipedia category which is the answer type
- NCcand: all entries under Wikipedia categories whose heads are WordNet-connected to the answer type
- NEcand: all entries whose head is WordNet-connected to the answer type
- Union: union of all the answer candidate sets listed above
- WikiAll: using all the Wikipedia entries in different types (upper bound of the coverage)

Model		Q with Focus and Wiki Ans					Q with Focus and Wiki Ans in 1000doc				
Atype	CandSet	ART	ORG	LOC	PRS	All	ART	ORG	LOC	PRS	All
WKtype	WKcand	12	27	49	91	179	12	25	45	76	158
CKtype	WKcand	12	28	49	91	180	12	26	45	76	159
KKtype	WKcand	12	28	49	91	180	12	26	45	76	159
KNtype	NCcand	13	28	51	84	176	13	27	49	71	160
KNtype	NEcand	15	29	54	85	183	15	27	52	71	165
Union		15	29	56	91	191	15	27	52	76	170
WikiAll		15	29	56	96	196	15	27	53	80	175

Table 3. Number of Questions Having Correct Answer Candidates with Different Methods

Atype	CandSet	ART	ORG	LOC	PRS	All
KKtype	WKcand	1551.2	1893.3	4461.7	2475.5	2520.3
KNtype	NCcand	1035.8	548.6	2774.6	676.8	970.5
KNtype	NEcand	531.4	400.9	699.1	514.0	512.4
WikiAll		11822.0	5707.1	21093.5	11190.5	11222.5

Table 4. Average Number of the Distinct Answer Candidates Found in Top 1000 Documents

WikiAll is our baseline model. We collected several Wikipedia infobox templates of and mapped them into the four question types. For example, when an entry has an infobox written in the format of "infobox:組織" (infobox:organization), it is an answer candidate to an ORGANIZATION question.

The left part of Table 3 gives the coverage of different candidate sets which contain correct answers. The right part of Table 3 gives the number of questions whose correct answers appear in the top 1000 relevant documents. All the methods have very similar coverage rates. But they proposed different candidate sets, because the union sets have the greatest coverage of correct answers.

Table 4 shows the average number of distinct answer candidates found in the 1000 relevant documents. We argue that more candidates will cause more noise. Apparently WikiAll has the most candidates. Averagely every question has 11,222.5 candidates to be scored thus is quite noisy.

We can see from Table 3 and 4 that KNtype+NEcand can successfully narrow down the size of candidates to be 512.4 in average but still has the best correct-answer coverage except the union method.

Note that we did not list the results of WNtype and CNtype, because they had worse experimental results than KNtype. Although WNtype and CNtype can capture more accurate answer types, unfortunately the correct answers are neither Wikipedia entries nor instances of the detected type.

4.4 Question Answering Performance

Table 5 and Table 6 show the performance of our QA system in MRR score and top-1 accuracy, where results in Table 6 were measured on all questions and Table 5 only on questions with explicit foci. The answer candidates for questions without foci were the entire WikiAll sets.

These two tables give the same conclusions. The union of the candidate sets achieves better performance than other models. It greatly outperformed WikiAll, which provided too much candidates.

Model	MRR					Top-1 accuracy				
	ART	ORG	LOC	PRS	All	ART	ORG	LOC	PRS	All
KKtype+WKcand	0.438	0.443	0.343	0.351	0.370	0.350	0.355	0.259	0.283	0.293
KNtype+NCcand	0.450	0.519	0.428	0.336	0.396	**0.400**	0.454	0.345	**0.295**	0.340
KNtype+NEcand	0.442	**0.582**	**0.452**	0.321	0.403	0.386	**0.499**	**0.411**	0.283	**0.356**
Union	**0.492**	0.490	0.449	**0.370**	**0.418**	**0.400**	0.387	0.345	0.292	0.329
WikiAll	0.229	0.319	0.299	0.272	0.282	0.150	0.194	0.207	0.177	0.185

Table 5. Performance of Answering Questions with QFocus

Model	MRR					Top-1 accuracy				
	ART	ORG	LOC	PRS	All	ART	ORG	LOC	PRS	All
KKtype+WKcand	0.438	0.433	0.340	0.361	0.371	0.350	0.333	0.246	0.288	0.288
KNtype+NCcand	0.450	0.528	0.452	0.358	0.415	**0.400**	0.455	0.348	**0.297**	0.341
KNtype+NEcand	0.442	**0.587**	0.458	0.340	0.414	0.350	**0.486**	**0.377**	0.296	**0.349**
Union	**0.492**	0.479	**0.470**	**0.378**	**0.426**	**0.400**	0.365	0.348	**0.297**	0.329
WikiAll	0.229	0.316	0.286	0.271	0.278	0.150	0.180	0.188	0.175	0.178

Table 6. Performance of Answering All Questions

In order to compare our work with previous NTCIR QA systems, we adapted our QA system (Lin and Liu, 2007) to use the union of answer candidates by our proposed models. The choice of using a typical QA system was based on the reason that our main interest was to observe the improvement when introducing new sets of answer candidates.

Table 7 shows the performance of our system comparing to the best teams in CLQA1 and CLQA2 (Lee *et al.*, 2007; Kwok *et al.*, 2007) according to 4 answer types. Our system outperforms CLQA best teams on ARTIFACT and ORGANIZATION types as we have expected. Although our methods were implemented on a baseline QA system, we believe that other QA systems can also be improved by our methods.

Note that our methods did not improve QA performance on PERSON and LOCATION types. We found that the CLQA questions were created from news articles and some of them were asking information about local events. It did not violate the design of ad hoc QA task (i.e. finding answers in a given corpus), but the answers were not world-wide famous so there were no Wikipedia entries introducing them. It reveals one weakness of our methods.

Atype	CLQA1		CLQA2		
	Our Work	ASQA	Our Work	ASQA	Pircs
ARTIFACT	**0.385**	0.159	**0.714**	0.286	0.429
ORGANIZATION	**0.556**	0.389	0.533	**0.563**	0.313
LOCATION	0.415	**0.457**	0.438	**0.875**	0.500
PERSON	0.375	**0.563**	0.422	**0.660**	0.575

Table 7. Comparison to the Best Teams in CLQA Tasks

5　Conclusion

This paper proposes a method to bridge Wikipedia and WordNet (together with other semantic resources) in order to find a proper-sized answer candidate sets inside Wikipedia. The experimental results showed that the union of the sets of answer candidates suggested by our methods could provide a suitable-sized set of answer candidates yet still improve a baseline QA system.

In our proposed QA system, an answer type is determined by finding a trailing substring of the question focus which is also a Wikipedia category. The question focus may be rephrased by synonyms (in WordNet or Wikipedia) before the answer type determination.

The answer candidate set is determined by collecting either all Wikipedia entries in the subtree under the answer type in the hierarchy of Wikipedia categories, or all entries under the categories which have heads related to the answer type in WordNet, or all entries having heads related to the answer type in WordNet. Our final system uses the union of these kinds of candidates and achieves the best performance among different models.

Although the experimental results seem promising, it is a pity that the dataset is too small and no other suitable benchmarks are available. We wish to find a different way to setup the experiments in the future in order to verify our conclusion with stronger evidence.

Adapting our methods to another language, such as English, is a good way to have larger experiment sets. English Wikipedia uses the same strategy to build hierarchies thus we can obtain answer candidates in the same way. WordNet itself is built in English thus synonym-rephrasing is also possible during answer type determination or candidate scoring. We would like to see if the proposed methods have similar conclusions in English in the future.

Reference

Sisay Fissaha Adafre and Josef van Genabith (2008) "Dublin City University at QA@CLEF 2008," *Proceedings of CLEF 2008 - 9th Workshop of the Cross-Language Evaluation Forum*, pp. 353-360.

Ali Mohamed Nabil Allam and Mohamed Hassan Haggag (2012) "The Question Answering Systems: A Survey," *International Journal of Research and Reviews in Information Sciences (IJRRIS)*, Vol. 2, No. 3, pp. 211-221.

David Buscaldi and Paolo Rosso (2006) "Mining Knowledge from Wikipedia from the Question Answering Task," *Proceedings of the 5th International Conference on Language Resources and Evaluation (LREC 2006)*, pp. 727-730.

Hoa Trang Dang, Diane Kelly, and Jimmy Lin (2007) "Overview of the TREC 2007 Question Answering Track," *Proceedings of TREC 2007*.

Ulrich Furbach, Ingo Glöckner, Hermann Helbig, and Björn Pelzer (2008) "Loganswer - a Deduction-Based Question Answering System," *Proceedings of the 4th international joint conference on Automated Reasoning, (IJCAR '08)*, pp. 139-146.

Sanda Harabagiu and Andrew Hickl (2006) "Methods for Using Textual Entailment in Open-Domain Question Answering," *Proceedings of the 21st International Conference on Computational Linguistics and the 44th annual meeting of the ACL*, pp. 905-912.

Dan Klein and Christopher D. Manning (2003) "Accurate Unlexicalized Parsing," *Proceedings of the 41st Meeting of the Association for Computational Linguistics*, pp. 423-430.

Kui-Lam Kwok, Peter Deng, and Norbert Dinstl (2007) "NTCIR-6 Monolingual Chinese and English-Chinese Cross-Lingual Question Answering Experiments using PIRCS," *Proceedings of NTCIR-6 Workshop Meeting*, pp. 190-197.

Cheng-Wei Lee, Min-Yuh Day, Cheng-Lung Sung, Yi-Hsun Lee, Mike Tian-Jian Jiang, Chia-Wei Wu, Cheng-Wei Shih, Yu-Ren Chen, and Wen-Lian Hsu (2007) "Chinese-Chinese and English-Chinese Question Answering with ASQA at NTCIR-6 CLQA," *Proceedings of NTCIR-6 Workshop Meeting*, pp. 175-181.

Cheng-Wei Lee, Min-Yuh Day, Cheng-Lung Sung, Yi-Hsun Lee, Tian-Jian Jiang, Chia-Wei Wu, Cheng-Wei Shih, Yu-Ren Chen, and Wen-Lian Hsu (2008) "Boosting Chinese Question Answering with Two Lightweight Methods: ABSPs and SCO-QAT," *ACM Transactions on Asian Language Information Processing (TALIP)*, Vol. 7, Issue 4, pp. 12:1-12:29.

Chuan-Jie Lin and Ren-Rui Liu (2008) "An Analysis of Multi-Focus Questions," *Proceedings of the 31st Annual International ACM SIGIR Conference on Research and Development in Information Retrieval (SIGIR 2008), Workshop on Focused Retrieval*, pp. 30-36.

Tomas Mikolov, Kai Chen, Greg Corrado, and Jeffrey Dean (2013) "Efficient Estimation of Word Representations in Vector Space," *Proceedings of the Workshop in the International Conference on Learning Representations (ICLR 2013)*.

Dan Moldovan, Christine Clark, Sanda Harabagiu, and Daniel Hodges (2007) "Cogex: A Semantically and Contextually Enriched Logic Prover for Question Answering," *Journal of Applied Logic*, Vol. 5, Issue 1, pp. 49-69.

David Nadeau and Satoshi Sekine (2007) "A survey of named entity recognition and classification," *Linguisticae Investigationes*, Vol. 30, No. 1, pp. 3-26.

Anselmo Peñas, Christina Unger, and Axel-Cyrille Ngonga (2014) "Overview of CLEF Question Answering Track 2014," *Information Access Evaluation. Multilinguality, Multimodality, and Interaction, Lecture Notes in Computer Science*, Vol. 8685, pp. 300-306.

Simone Paolo Ponzetto and Michael Strube (2007) "Knowledge Derived from Wikipedia for Computing Semantic Relatedness," *Journal of Artificial Intelligence Research* (*JAIR*), Vol. 30, pp. 181-212.

Bogdan Sacaleanu, Constantin Orasan, Christian Spurk, Shiyan Ou, Oscar Ferrandez, Milen Kouylekov, and Matteo Negri (2008) "Entailment-Based Question Answering for Structured Data," *Proceedings of 22nd International Conference on Computational Linguistics (COLING 2008)*, pp. 173-176.

Tetsuya Sakai, Hideki Shima, Noriko Kando, Ruihua Song, Chuan-Jie Lin, Teruko Mitamura, Miho Sugimito, and Cheng-Wei Lee (2010) "Overview of NTCIR-8 ACLIA IR4QA," *Proceedings of the 8th NTCIR Workshop Meeting on Evaluation of Information Access Technologies: Information Retrieval, Question Answering, and Cross-Lingual Information Access (NTCIR-8)*, pp. 63-93.

Juliano Efson Sales, André Freitas, Brian Davis, and Siegfried Handschuh (2016) "A Compositional-Distributional Semantic Model for Searching Complex Entity Categories," *Proceedings of the 5th Joint Conference on Lexical and Computational Semantics (*SEM)*, pp. 199-208.

Yutaka Sasaki, Hsin-Hsi Chen, Kuang-hua Chen, and Chuan-Jie Lin (2007) "Overview of the NTCIR-5 Cross-Lingual Question Answering Task (CLQA1)," *Proceedings of NTCIR-5 Workshop Meeting*, pp. 175-185.

Yutaka Sasaki, Chuan-Jie Lin, Kuang-hua Chen, and Hsin-Hsi Chen (2007) "Overview of the NTCIR-6 Cross-Lingual Question Answering (CLQA) Task," *Proceedings of NTCIR-6*, pp. 153-163.

Ulli Waltinger, Alexa Breuing, and Ipke Wachsmuth (2011) "Interfacing Virtual Agents with Collaborative Knowledge: Open Domain Question Answering Using Wikipedia-Based Topic Models," *Proceedings of the 22nd International Joint Conference on Artificial Intelligence (IJCAI-11)*, pp. 1896-1902.

Large-Scale Acquisition of Commonsense Knowledge via a Quiz Game on a Dialogue System

Naoki Otani[1]   **Daisuke Kawahara**[1]   **Sadao Kurohashi**[1]

Nobuhiro Kaji[2]   **Manabu Sassano**[2]

[1]Graduate School of Informatics, Kyoto University, Kyoto, Japan
[2]Yahoo Japan Corporation, Tokyo, Japan

`otani.naoki.65v@st.kyoto-u.ac.jp` `{dk,kuro}@i.kyoto-u.ac.jp`
`{nkaji,msassano}@yahoo-corp.jp`

Abstract

Commonsense knowledge is essential for fully understanding language in many situations. We acquire large-scale commonsense knowledge from humans using a game with a purpose (GWAP) developed on a smartphone spoken dialogue system. We transform the manual knowledge acquisition process into an enjoyable quiz game and have collected over 150,000 unique commonsense facts by gathering the data of more than 70,000 players over eight months. In this paper, we present a simple method for maintaining the quality of acquired knowledge and an empirical analysis of the knowledge acquisition process. To the best of our knowledge, this is the first work to collect large-scale knowledge via a GWAP on a widely-used spoken dialogue system.

1 Introduction

Large-scale knowledge is an essential resource in many natural language processing (NLP) applications. There have long been efforts devoted to collecting *commonsense knowledge*, *i.e.*, general knowledge that every person knows (Zang et al., 2013). We rely on such prior knowledge to understand languages. For example, consider the sentence "She went to get strawberries." A human might think she went to the refrigerator in the kitchen or a supermarket in the neighborhood. Computers, however, do not know that strawberries would be stored in refrigerators. This paper presents a methodology for acquiring large-scale commonsense knowledge from humans.

Early work on commonsense knowledge acquisition includes the Cyc project (Lenat, 1995), where a small group of human annotators organized resources. Manually curated resources are of high quality but require significant cost and time to build. Thus, several studies have automatically constructed knowledge bases on existing resources such as semi-structured or unstructured texts (for example, (Tandon et al., 2014)). However, commonsense knowledge is so clear for every person that it is often omitted in a text (Gordon and Van Durme, 2013). For instance, we rarely state in a text that strawberries are stored in refrigerators. Rather, we often talk about a major production region for strawberries. Therefore, manual effort is still required to build commonsense knowledge bases.

To reduce the cost of manual knowledge acquisition, some studies explored the use of crowdsourcing, a process that requests various tasks of non-expert workers on the Internet. The Open Mind Common Sense (OMCS) project (Liu and Singh, 2004; Speer and Havasi, 2012) recruited volunteers on the Internet and constructed *ConceptNet*, a large collection of commonsense knowledge such as (cake, *AtLocation*, supermarket). Whereas participants in the OMCS projects entered the commonsense knowledge in Web forms, some studies have transformed the knowledge acquisition process into a type of enjoyable game, called *games with a purpose* (GWAP) (von Ahn et al., 2006; Lieberman et al., 2007; Kuo et al., 2009; Nakahara, 2011; Herdağdelen and Barobni, 2012; Kuo and Hsu, 2011). The advantage of a GWAP is that it is more attractive to humans than the standard annotation processes and is able to collect accurate resources as a side effect of their enjoyment of the games.

Proceedings of the Open Knowledge Base and Question Answering (OKBQA) Workshop,
pages 11–20, Osaka, Japan, December 11 2016.

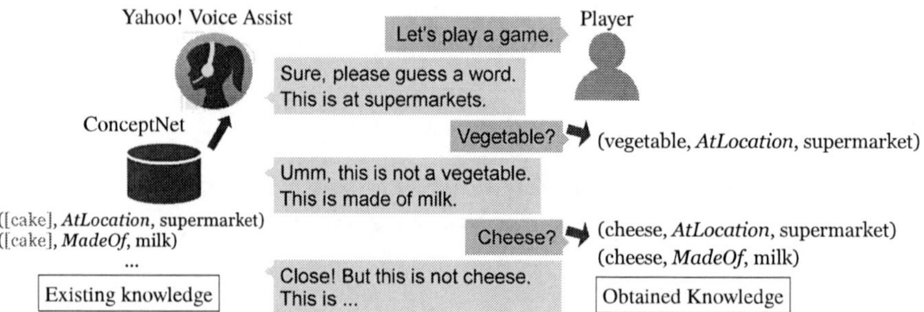

Figure 1: **Illustration of the quiz game.** A player is given clues about a certain word to be guessed. The clues are generated from existing knowledge in ConceptNet. We learn new knowledge from the player's guesses given the clues.

We developed a quiz game shown in Figure 1 as a module in the widely-used Japanese smartphone app, *Yahoo! Voice Assist*[1] (hereafter Voice Assist), which is a Siri-like spoken dialogue system that has been downloaded to more than 2.5 million devices. Although it is usually hard to get GWAP participants over the long term, our game is able to reach greater numbers of users than previous studies.

The quiz game follows the same framework as the previous work by Nakahara (2011), in which players are given clues about a certain word. From the players' incorrect guesses, we can obtain knowledge about the clues. For example, a hint "this is made of milk" is given to a player. The expected answer is a cake, but we can learn that "cheese is made of milk" when the player answers "cheese" in response to the hint.

Spoken dialogue systems on smartphones such as Siri and Cortana have attracted many industrial and research interests in recent years. They are promising as platforms of knowledge acquisition from humans because they have a large number of users. Furthermore, acquired knowledge is useful for developing sophisticated dialogue systems and attracting more users. Consequently, we can collect more knowledge from more users. Additionally, enjoyable user interaction without any goals is important. Even in a task-oriented dialogue system, Jiang et al. (2015) report that about 20% of user logs are chat, and some studies report that games on a dialogue system improve user engagement with the system (Kobayashi et al., 2015; Sano et al., 2016).

As the obtained knowledge contains incorrect facts, we aggregate facts collected from multiple players to determine the correct facts. Such incorrect facts come from players' guesses that are not relevant to the hints and automatic speech recognition (ASR) errors, which is a characteristic of spoken dialogue systems. To address these problems, it is not sufficient to only consider the number of players who give the same facts, as previous studies have done (von Ahn et al., 2006; Kuo et al., 2009; Nakahara, 2011). We present a method to reduce the ASR errors and estimate the confidence scores of facts.

We released the game in December 2015 and have collected more than 150,000 unique facts over eight months. The number of unique players was 70,000 in total, which is much larger than those of previous studies, for example, 6,899 players over six months for the game by Kuo et al. (2009). We evaluated the quality of the collected knowledge in two ways. We first evaluated the scoring method of the facts using crowdsourced annotations, and then manually evaluated samples of the collected knowledge. The results show that our quiz game is an effective way to acquire large-scale commonsense knowledge.

Our contributions are summarized as follows.

1. We collected large-scale, high quality knowledge from a quiz game on a dialogue system that has many users. We will make the collected resources publicly available.
2. We present a method to reduce ASR errors and maintain the quality of acquired knowledge.

2   Related Work

Research in knowledge base construction has contributed to the success of many applications including question answering and information extraction. Some knowledge bases are manually constructed,

---

[1] `http://v-assist.yahoo.co.jp` (in Japanese)

and others are automatically constructed from texts and existing resources. Automatically constructed large-scale knowledge bases include Freebase (Bollacker et al., 2008), which was constructed from Wikipedia's texts and existing resources such as WordNet. Freebase has been successfully used in many NLP tasks.

Whereas most large-scale knowledge bases focus on relations between named entities, we focus on commonsense knowledge, which has a wider range. The Cyc Project (Lenat, 1995), an early work on commonsense knowledge acquisition, recruited a small group of annotators to construct a knowledge base.

Manually curated resources are accurate but expensive to build. Several studies have attempted to construct knowledge bases automatically. For example, Tandon et al. (2014) extracted knowledge from WordNet and Web texts. However, commonsense knowledge is likely to be omitted from texts because it is assumed that every person knows such knowledge (Gordon and Van Durme, 2013). Li et al. (2016) addressed this problem using knowledge base completion, in which existing knowledge is used to acquire more knowledge. However, their method needs some amount of existing knowledge as a seed. Thus, manual effort is still required.

Crowdsourcing, which is a process that requests various tasks of non-expert workers on the Internet, can be used to reduce the cost of the manual process. The OMCS project (Liu and Singh, 2004; Speer and Havasi, 2012) collected commonsense knowledge by recruiting many volunteers on the Internet. The resulting knowledge base is called ConceptNet,[2] which we use and extend in our study.

Some studies transform the manual acquisition process into an enjoyable game, called a GWAP, to motivate players to participate in knowledge acquisition. GWAPs are a form of crowdsourcing[3] and have been used for validating (Herdağdelen and Barobni, 2012; Vannella et al., 2014; Machida et al., 2016) and collecting (von Ahn et al., 2006; Lieberman et al., 2007; Kuo et al., 2009; Nakahara, 2011; Kuo and Hsu, 2011; Nakahara and Yamada, 2013) language resources.

A word-guessing game was designed by von Ahn et al. (2006) to collect a large amount of knowledge within a short time and at a low cost. GWAPs have also been exploited to acquire knowledge in Chinese (Kuo et al., 2009; Kuo and Hsu, 2011) and Japanese (Nakahara, 2011; Nakahara and Yamada, 2013). The collected knowledge was registered in ConceptNet. Although it is generally hard to gather many players, our GWAP can reach many more users than previous studies because it is built on a running spoken dialogue system.

Spoken dialogue systems on smartphones have been attracting much industrial and research interest in recent years. Several studies report that enjoyable user interactions are beneficial for dialogue systems (Jiang et al., 2015; Kobayashi et al., 2015; Sano et al., 2016).

3 Rapid Knowledge Acquisition from Quiz Game

We use a quiz game on a spoken dialogue system to obtain large-scale, high-quality commonsense knowledge from many human players.

3.1 Japanese ConceptNet

Our knowledge acquisition method follows the scheme of ConceptNet (Speer and Havasi, 2012). In ConceptNet, knowledge is expressed as a triple of two concepts and a relation linking them, where a concept is a word or a short phrase, and a relation consists of about 30 relations such as *IsA*, *Causes*, or *Antonym*. We call a triple a *fact*, and the two concepts are called a *head* and *tail*, respectively.

Japanese ConceptNet has 95,468 facts in total.[4] We ignore facts obtained using the game by Nakahara (2011) with a weight of one (*i.e.*, only one player provided this fact) because these facts are likely to be inaccurate . The filtered ConceptNet has only 46,427 unique facts, and most of them are lexical knowledge (*e.g.*, *Antonym* and *DerivedFrom*). In contrast, Japanese WordNet,[5] for example, has 93,834

---

[2] `http://conceptnet5.media.mit.edu`
[3] For more information about crowdsourcing, readers can refer to (Law and von Ahn, 2011).
[4] From a snapshot taken on Sept. 10th, 2015 at `http://conceptnet5.media.mit.edu/downloads/20150910/`.
[5] `http://compling.hss.ntu.edu.sg/wnja/index.en.html`

words and many relations linking them. Thus, collecting more commonsense facts is essential to making them at least as useful in NLP tasks as WordNet is.

We only consider the filtered ConceptNet in the rest of this paper. Note that words in heads and tails are normalized into their representative forms (*e.g.*, { みかん mikan, ミカン mikan, 蜜柑 mikan} (orange) → みかん mikan (orange)) given by the morphological analyzer JUMAN++ (Morita et al., 2015).

3.2 Building a Quiz from using ConceptNet

We collect commonsense knowledge from many people. To motivate them, we transform the knowledge acquisition process into an enjoyable quiz game, where human players are given several hints about a certain word to be guessed, and we acquire knowledge from players' guesses. The hints are easily generated from existing knowledge in ConceptNet. Figure 1 shows examples. "This is at supermarkets" and "this is made of milk" are generated from the facts (cake, *AtLocation*, supermarket) and (cake *MadeOf*, milk), respectively. The word to be guessed (hereafter *keyword*) is "cake."

From the player's guesses, we can obtain knowledge about each relation and tail pair. For instance, we can learn that "cheese is made of milk" when the player answered "cheese" to the hint "this is made of milk." Note that we only hide the head of a fact and let players guess the word that fits with its relation and tail because this allows players to give diverse answers. For example, we use "X is made of milk" rather than "cake is made of X" to obtain many different responses.

If the player fails to guess the keyword, another hint is selected at random and given to the player. Our game gives up to five hints,[6] and 15 facts can be acquired from a player's guesses. We call the distance between a player's guess and a given hint the *hint distance*. The hint distances of (cheese, *MadeOf*, milk) and (cheese, *AtLocation*, supermarket) in Figure 1 are one and two, respectively.

The game is implemented as a part of the chat function of Voice Assist, which is the Japanese spoken dialogue system on smartphones, and is executed as follows:

1. A player utters a sentence such as "ゲームしよう" ("Let's play a game"), and the game session starts.
2. A keyword is selected randomly.
3. A hint about the keyword is drawn. The hint sentence is generated using predefined templates.
4. Given the hint, the player utters his/her guess.
5. If the guess matches the keyword, the game session ends and the system returns to the normal dialogue processing mode; otherwise the system returns to step 3 to add more hints to the quiz until the number of hints reaches its limit. If the number of hints reaches its limit, the system ends the game and returns to the normal dialogue processing mode.

To build a list of keywords and hints to be used in the game, we extracted the heads of facts in ConceptNet that have more than five facts with two or more different relations. Finally, the authors and developers of Voice Assist selected appropriate keywords and hints from the candidates. Note that we did not use lexical knowledge.

3.3 Reducing ASR Errors

Player's utterances are likely to suffer from ASR errors because they are not accompanied by any context that is helpful for recognizing words. Table 1(a) provides examples. In Japanese, for example, "cheese" (チーズ chîzu) is sometimes recognized as "a map" (地図 chizu). To alleviate this problem, we automatically identify ASR errors and rewrite them into their correct forms.

We first identify ASR error pairs and the correct form based on pronunciations. We transcribe the collected words into *rōmaji*,[7] which represents their pronunciations, and calculate the string similarities between the transcribed words that were given in response to the same hint. We define the string similarity of transcribed strings X and Y as $1 - \frac{L(X,Y)}{\max\{|X|,|Y|\}}$, where L denotes the Levenshtein distance and $|\cdot|$ denotes the length of the string. The pair of words is considered to be identical if the similarity is higher

---

[6] We followed Nakahara (2011) and determined the maximum number of hints.

[7] We used **KAKASI** (http://kakasi.namazu.org/index.html.en) to convert a word into *rōmaji*.

Keyword	Recognized facts	Intended head
cake	(地図 chizu (map), *MadeOf*, milk)	チーズ chîzu (cheese)
orange	(佐藤 satô (Japanese family name), *HasProperty*, sweet)	砂糖 satô (sugar)
kitchen knife	(校長 kôchô (school principal), *UsedFor*, cut)	包丁 hôchô (kitchen knife)

(a) ASR errors: Intended heads were given by the authors.

Turn	Hint / Guess	Obtained facts
Hint (H) 1	This is herbivore.	
Guess (G) 1	Sheep.	(sheep, *HasProperty*, herbivore)
H2	This is yellow.	
G2	Tiger.	**(tiger, *HasProperty*, herbivore)**, (tiger, *HasProperty*, yellow)

(b) Hint distances: The hint distance of (tiger, *HasProperty*, herbivore) is two, and the others are one.

Table 1: **Illustration of inaccurate facts obtained from the quiz game.** For simplicity, only English translations are reported for some words.

than 0.7.[8] For example, チーズ (cheese) and 地図 (map) are identical because the their pronunciations, chîzu and chizu, are sufficiently similar.

Next, we rewrite the identical words to the correct words. We do not yet know which of the words is the correct form. The key to determining the correct form is that a player's guess will be semantically similar to the keyword because the player is attempting to answer the keyword in the game. We take cheese (チーズ chîzu) and a map (地図 chizu) given in response to the hint "this is made of milk," for example. Assume the keyword is "cake." We calculate the cosine similarities between the word vectors (Mikolov et al., 2013) of the guesses and the keyword, obtaining sim(cheese, cake) = 0.65, and sim(map, cake) = 0.13. Indeed, (cheese, *MadeOf*, milk) is correct, and (map, *MadeOf*, milk) is incorrect.

We assume that the word whose word vector is more similar to that of the keyword is correct. Thus, 地図 (map) is rewritten to チーズ (cheese), whose semantic similarity to the keyword, *i.e.*, sim(cheese, cake), is higher than sim(map, cake).

3.4 Aggregation of Acquired Knowledge

The quality of the acquired knowledge is not always good, and we must aggregate multiple facts obtained from the players to learn correct knowledge. To this end, we consider the following three aspects of the knowledge acquisition process from the quiz game.

1. Similarly to previous studies (von Ahn et al., 2006; Kuo and Hsu, 2011; Herdağdelen and Barobni, 2012; Nakahara, 2011), we assume that facts given by many players are likely to be correct. We use P_f to denote the set of players that answered the head of fact f. If P_f consists of many players, f obtains a high score.

2. A fact whose hint distance is large is less reliable than a fact whose hint distance is small because players focus on the last hint and tend to ignore earlier hints (see Table 1(b) for example). Thus, we weight frequency by hint distance (Section 3.2). The distance of fact f given by player p is denoted by $d(f, p)$. We weight fact f given by player p by $w_d(f, p) = g^{-d(f,p)}$, where g is a hyperparameter.

3. As explained in the previous section, a correct word is likely to be semantically similar to the keyword. Thus, we can also use the semantic similarity between a player's guess and keyword as prior knowledge during scoring. We define the weight of fact f as $w_s(f) = (\mathrm{sim}(f_{\text{head}}, f_{\text{keyword}}) + 1)/2$, where sim is the cosine similarity between word vectors, and f_{head} and f_{keyword} are the head and keyword of fact f, respectively.

Our goal is to give a high score to correct facts (e.g., (cheese, *MadeOf*, milk)) and a low score to incorrect facts (e.g., (noodle, *MadeOf*, cheese)). Combining the ideas above, we define the score of fact f as

$$\sum_{p \in P_f} w_d(f, p) \times w_s(f).$$

---

[8]We empirically determined the threshold using a small set of word pairs.

Unique players	Games	Utterances	Unique facts
74,375	206,305	588,189	155,683

Table 2: **Data collected by the quiz game from December 2015 to August 2016.**

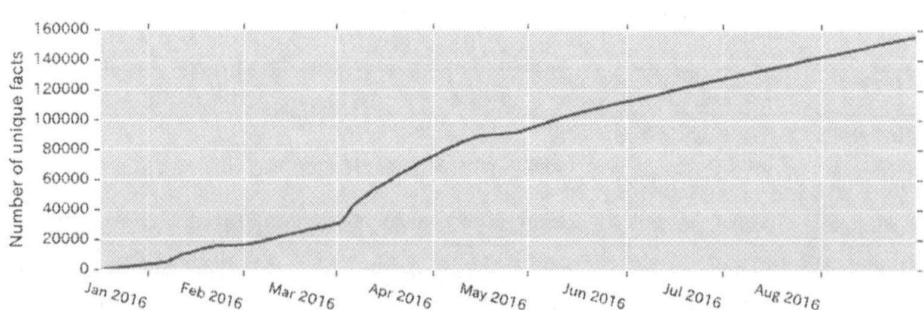

Figure 2: **Amount of newly acquired knowledge.** 98% of the facts did not exist in ConceptNet.

4 Empirical Evaluation

4.1 Knowledge Acquisition Speed

We created quizzes by following the procedure in Section 3.2 and released the game to a subset of the Voice Assist users in December 2015 and all users in March 2016. Table 2 shows the statistics of the collected data. At its peak, 1,300 unique players participated per day. These numbers are much larger than those of previous studies (for instance, 6,899 players over six months for the pet game (Kuo et al., 2009)).

Figure 2 shows the amount of newly acquired knowledge (*i.e.*, a cumulative sum of the number of unique facts). By March 2016, we had collected over 30,000 unique facts using only 92 hints. Because we increased the number of hints to 181 and published the game to all users in March 2016, the acquisition speed was accelerated. We obtained over 60,000 unique facts in March and 20,000 unique facts per month after that. There are 805 facts in the Japanese ConceptNet that have the same (*relation*, tail) as the hints added in March 2016. Surprisingly, 70% of them were obtained within the first nine days of our quiz game.

We cleaned the collected logs before this analysis because they contained meaningless utterances. **(1) Time out:** We discarded the rest of the utterances if the utterance interval exceeded one minute. **(2) Activation of Voice Assist functions:** If players uttered a command for one of the other functions such as calling, weather information or navigation, we considered it to be the last utterance of the session and discarded the rest of the utterances. **(3) Trivial utterances:** Utterances matching trivial patterns defined by the authors were discarded. **(4) Part-of-speech (POS):** Heads that do not meet a constraint on the POS of the relation type were filtered out from the extracted facts, where we used JUMAN++ (Morita et al., 2015) for morphological analysis. The constraints can be found in Speer and Havasi (2012).

4.2 Evaluation Using Crowdsourcing

We use crowdsourced judgments as the gold standard for evaluating the collected knowledge. We recruited crowd workers on Yahoo! Crowdsourcing[9] and evaluated 6,669 facts that were collected from multiple players. The facts were sampled from the data collected up to the end of February 2016. The workers answered whether a given fact was correct or not. We requested the judgments of five workers for each fact and aggregated them using the multi-class minimax entropy algorithm (Zhou et al., 2014).

The facts that were labeled as true consisted of 54% of all the facts. This is lower than those of previous studies because our game suffered from ASR errors. To obtain correct knowledge from such noisy collected facts, we needed to aggregate them and estimate confidence scores for each fact.

In this analysis, we validate the performance of the scoring method explained in Section 3.4 in terms of ROC-AUC, performing 3-fold cross validation on the evaluation set. To calculate a weight based on hint distances, we determined g by doing a grid search over $\{2, 4, 8, 16\}$, searching for the values that

---

[9]http://crowdsourcing.yahoo.co.jp/

Reducing ASR errors	baseline		+ hint distance		+ semantic similarity		+ both	
		✓		✓		✓		✓
	0.695	0.707	0.752	0.769	0.709	0.718	0.764	**0.777**

Table 3: **ROC-AUC of estimated confidence scores.** Note that the number of evaluated facts is different before and after ASR error reduction using the method explained in Section 3.3 (6,669 and 5,669 facts, respectively).

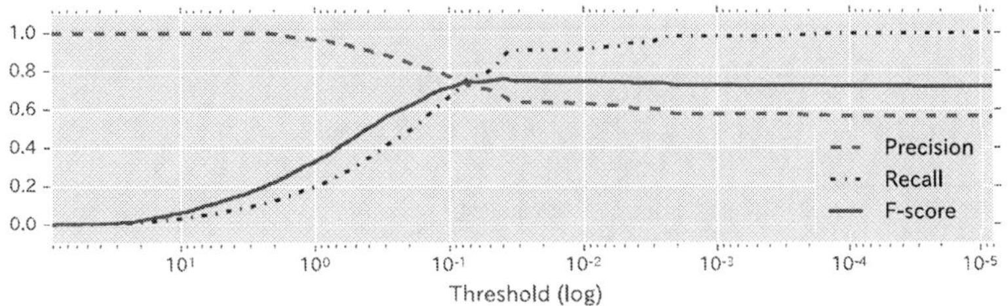

Figure 3: **Relationship between precision/recall/F-score and score threshold.**

maximized the ROC-AUC on the development set. We used word vectors of 500 dimensions that were trained on 9.8 billion Japanese sentences crawled from the Web.

Table 3 shows the ROC-AUC for the evaluation data. It indicates that when facts are ranked by hint distances and semantic similarity to keywords, the performance is better than only considering the number of players that answered the fact, as previous studies did.

4.3 Case Study of Knowledge Acquisition

Although the analysis using crowdsourcing in the previous section is efficient for validating the performance of the scoring methods, it is not sufficient for evaluating the quality of acquired knowledge. Thus, we need a detailed analysis of the acquired knowledge. We first divided the facts into four groups based on their scores and evaluated 100 facts for each group manually.

Figure 3 shows the precision and recall corresponding to thresholds on the scores. The F-score value reaches the highest at around 0.1. Hence, we consider the following four groups: (A) 100 highest-scoring facts, (B) 100 highest-scoring facts whose scores are below 1, (C) 100 lowest-scoring facts whose scores are above 0.1, and (D) 100 highest-scoring facts whose scores are below 0.1.

As the validity of a fact depends on the context in which it is used, we classified a fact into ASR errors and five classes: (5) always true, (4) true in many contexts, (3) true in several contexts, (2) true in only a few contexts, and (1) false.

Table 4 shows the evaluation results. We observe that the top-ranked facts contain knowledge that is true in general contexts, whereas the facts in the low-scoring groups include many context-dependent or incorrect facts. Table 5 provides examples for each group. In group (A), most of the 100 facts contain keywords or their synonyms and already exist in ConceptNet. This is because players tried to answer the keywords in the game. In contrast, 61, 90, and 92 out of 100 facts do not exist in ConceptNet in groups (B), (C), and (D), respectively.

As we expected, our quiz game obtained knowledge that is not likely to appear in texts. For example, (ladle, *AtLocation*, kitchen), (restaurant, *RelatedTo*, work), and (marriage proposal, *RelatedTo*, meal) cannot be found in Wikipedia, a corpus often used for knowledge acquisition.

However, low-scoring groups (C) and (D) contain some incorrect facts. The false facts include (Wu long tea, *MadeOf*, beans) in (C) and (tiger, *HasProperty*, herbivore) in (D). ASR errors appear most in group (C) because their hint distances are close to zero even though their frequencies and semantic similarities to keywords are low. Tackling these problems is left for future work.

4.4 Discussion

Our game gives a hint (*relation*, tail) to players and only obtains the head corresponding to the hint (Section 3.2). If the number of collected facts increases, we can analyze this knowledge for further details. Suppose we obtained the head "strawberry" from two hints "this is at supermarkets" and "this is

Group	5	4	3	2	1	ASR error
(A)	93	5	2	0	0	0
(B)	85	9	4	1	0	1
(C)	48	11	13	8	7	13
(D)	50	12	14	11	9	4

Table 4: **Evaluation results.**

	Keyword	Collected fact	Score	Judgment
(A)	hair dryer	(ドライヤー (hair dryer), *UsedFor*, 髪を乾かす (dry hair))	93.22	5
	hair dryer	(ハサミ (scissors), *AtLocation* 床屋 (barbershop))	15.27	5
	TV	(テレビ (TV), *AtLocation*, リビングルーム (living room))	12.96	4
(B)	money	(バット (bat) *MadeOf*, 金属 (metal))	0.987	4
	kitchen knife	(おたま (ladle), *AtLocation*, キッチン (kitchen))	0.911	5
	cafe	(レストラン (restaurant), *RelatedTo*, 仕事 (work))	0.803	3
(C)	cafe	(プロポーズ (marriage proposal), *RelatedTo*, 食事 (meal))	0.107	4
	cellphone	(テレビ (TV), *IsA*, 電話 (telephone))	0.105	2
	coffee	(ウーロン茶 (Wu long tea), *MadeOf*, 豆 (beans))	0.106	1
(D)	cake	(コーヒー牛乳 (coffee-flavored milk), *Causes*, 虫歯 (tooth decay))	0.099	4
	farmer	(おまわりさん (police officer), *IsA*, 仕事 (job))	0.098	5
	giraffe	(虎 (tiger) *HasProperty*, 草食 (herbivore))	0.098	1

Table 5: **Examples of collected facts.**

at farms." We can undertake further analyses such as comparing the frequencies of (strawberry, *AtLocation*, supermarket) and (strawberry, *AtLocation*, farm) to learn where people mostly think strawberries are. This would be beneficial for computers to understand humans' social communications.

We obtained more than 60,000 facts within a month using about 200 hints in March 2016. We expect to collect millions of items of knowledge over a year by continuously updating the hints. The collected resources will be freely available.

5 Conclusion

We developed a quiz game as a module in a widely used Japanese spoken dialogue system to obtain large-scale and high quality commonsense knowledge from many humans. We released the game in December 2016 and so far have collected over 150,000 unique facts from more than 70,000 players. In this paper, we reported the speed and quality of the knowledge acquisition process using the dialogue system quiz game. We also addressed the problem of aggregating the collected facts to obtain correct knowledge. We presented a simple scoring method that considers hint distances and semantic similarities between a player's guesses and the answer of the quiz. The experiments showed that when facts are ranked by using the scoring method, the performance is better than when only the number of players that answered the fact is considered, as previous studies did.

As future work, we will develop further acquisition and validation methodologies to obtain accurate commonsense facts. ASR errors are hard to avoid in a spoken dialogue system, and we must develop a more sophisticated approach to tackle this problem. Furthermore, although our current quiz game selects a quiz and hint at random, it would be more effective to select them based on a strategy. For example, Kuo and Hsu (2011) attempted to utilize the English ConceptNet to generate effective quiz games.

We will collect additional knowledge by updating the quizzes continuously, and expect that the number of acquired facts will reach more than one million in the near future, which would be significantly beneficial for various Japanese NLP applications.

Acknowledgments

We would like to thank participants in our game and developers of Yahoo! Voice Assist. We are also thankful for the valuable comments from the anonymous reviewers. This research was supported by the Leading Graduates Schools Program, "Collaborative Graduate Program in Design" by the Ministry of Education, Culture, Sports, Science and Technology, Japan.

References

Kurt Bollacker, Colin Evans, Praveen Paritosh, Tim Sturge, and Jamie Taylor. 2008. Freebase: A collaboratively created graph database for structuring human knowledge. In *Proceedings of the 2008 ACM SIGMOD International Conference on Management of Data (SIGMOD)*, pages 1247–1249, New York, New York, USA, May. ACM Press.

Jonathan Gordon and Benjamin Van Durme. 2013. Reporting bias and knowledge acquisition. In *Proceedings of The 3rd Workshop on Automated Knowledge Base Construction (AKBC)*. ACM Press, October.

Amaç Herdağdelen and Marco Barobni. 2012. Bootstrapping a game with a purpose for commonsense collection. *ACM Transactions on Intelligent Systems and Technology*, 3(4):1–24.

Jiepu Jiang, Ahmed Hassan Awadallah, Rosie Jones, Umut Ozertem, Imed Zitouni, Ranjitha Gurunath Kulkarni, and Omar Zia Khan. 2015. Automatic online evaluation of intelligent assistants. In *Proceedings of the 24th International Conference on World Wide Web (WWW)*, pages 506–516, New York, New York, USA, May. ACM Press.

Hayato Kobayashi, Kaori Tanio, and Manabu Sassano. 2015. Effects of game on user engagement with spoken dialogue system. In *Proceedings of the 16th Annual Meeting of the Special Interest Group on Discourse and Dialogue (SIGDIAL)*, pages 422–426, Prague, Czech Republic, September. Association for Computational Linguistics.

Yen-Ling Kuo and Jane Yung-Jen Hsu. 2011. Resource-bounded crowd-sourcing of commonsense knowledge. In *Proceedings of the Twenty-Second International Joint Conference on Artificial Intelligence (IJCAI)*, pages 2470–2475, Barcelona, Spain, July. AAAI Press.

Yen-ling Kuo, Jong-Chuan Lee, Kai-yang Chiang, Rex Wang, Edward Shen, Cheng-wei Chan, and Jane Yung-jen Hsu. 2009. Community-based game design: Experiments on social games for commonsense data collection. In *Proceedings of the ACM SIGKDD Workshop on Human Computation (HCOMP)*, pages 15–22, Paris, France, June. ACM Press.

Edith Law and Luis von Ahn. 2011. *Human computation*, volume 5 of *Synthesis Lectures on Artificial Intelligence and Machine Learning*. Morgan & Claypool Publishers.

Douglas B. Lenat. 1995. Cyc: a large-scale investment in knowledge infrastructure. *Communications of the ACM*, 38(11):33–38.

Xiang Li, Aynaz Taheri, Lifu Tu, and Kevin Gimpel. 2016. Commonsense knowledge base completion. In *Proceedings of the 54th Annual Meeting of the Association for Computational Linguistics (ACL)*, Berlin, Germany, August. Association for Computational Linguistics.

Henry Lieberman, Dustin a Smith, and Alea Teeters. 2007. Common consensus: a web-based game for collecting commonsense goals. In *Proceedings of IUI 2007 Workshop on Common Sense for Intelligent Interfaces*, Honolulu, Hawaii, January. ACM Press.

Hugo Liu and Push Singh. 2004. Conceptnet — a practical commonsense reasoning tool-kit. *BT Technology Journal*, 22(4):211–226.

Yuichiro Machida, Daisuke Kawahara, Sadao Kurohashi, and Manabu Sassano. 2016. Design of word association games using dialog systems for acquisition of word association knowledge. In *Proceedings of the 5th Workshop on Automated Knowledge Base Construction (AKBC)*, pages 86–91, San Diego, CA, USA, June. Association for Computational Linguistics.

Tomas Mikolov, Ilya Sutskever, Kai Chen, Greg S. Corrado, and Jeff Dean. 2013. Distributed representations of words and phrases and their compositionality. In *Advances in Neural Information Processing Systems 26 (NIPS)*, pages 3111–3119, Stateline, Nevada, USA, December. MIT Press.

Hajime Morita, Daisuke Kawahara, and Sadao Kurohashi. 2015. Morphological analysis for unsegmented languages using recurrent neural network language model. In *Proceedings of the 2015 Conference on Empirical Methods in Natural Language Processing (EMNLP)*, pages 2292–2297, Lisbon, Portugal, September. Association for Computational Linguistics.

Kazuhiro Nakahara and Shigeo Yamada. 2013. Social game the test for Japanesenes for common-sense knowledge acquisition (in Japanese). *Unisys Technology Review*, 32(4):389–401.

Kazuhiro Nakahara. 2011. Development and evaluation of a web-based game for common-sense knowledge acquisition in Japan (in Japanese). *Unisys Technology Review*, 30(4):295–305.

Shumpei Sano, Nobuhiro Kaji, and Manabu Sassano. 2016. Prediction of prospective user engagement with intelligent assistants. In *Proceedings of the 54th Annual Meeting of the Association for Computational Linguistics (ACL)*, pages 1203–1212, Berlin, Germany, August. Association for Computational Linguistics.

Robert Speer and Catherine Havasi. 2012. Representing general relational knowledge in conceptnet 5. In Nicoletta Calzolari, Khalid Choukri, Thierry Declerck, Mehmet Uur Doan, Bente Maegaard, Joseph Mariani, Asuncion Moreno, Jan Odijk, and Stelios Piperidis, editors, *Proceedings of the Eighth International Conference on Language Resources and Evaluation (LREC)*, pages 3679–3686, Istanbul, Turkey, May. European Language Resources Association.

Niket Tandon, Gerard de Melo, Fabian Suchanek, and Gerhard Weikum. 2014. Webchild: Harvesting and organizing commonsense knowledge from the web. In *Proceedings of the 7th ACM international conference on Web search and data mining (WSDM)*, pages 523–532, New York, New York, USA, February. ACM Press.

Daniele Vannella, David Jurgens, Daniele Scarfini, Domenico Toscani, and Roberto Navigli. 2014. Validating and extending semantic knowledge bases using video games with a purpose. In *Proceedings of the 52nd Annual Meeting of the Association for Computational Linguistics (ACL)*, pages 1294–1304, Baltimore, Maryland, June. Association for Computational Linguistics.

Luis von Ahn, Mihir Kedia, and Manuel Blum. 2006. Verbosity: A game for collecting common-sense facts. In *Proceedings of the SIGCHI Conference on Human Factors in Computing Systems (CHI)*, pages 75–79, Montréal, Québec, Canada., April. ACM Press.

Liangjun Zang, Cong Cao, Yanan Cao, Yuming Wu, and Cungen Cao. 2013. A survey of commonsense knowledge acquisition. *Journal of Computer Science and Technology*, 28(4):689–719, July.

Dengyong Zhou, Qiang Liu, John Platt, and Christopher Meek. 2014. Aggregating ordinal labels from crowds by minimax conditional entropy. In *Proceedings of The 31st International Conference on Machine Learning (ICML)*, pages 262–270, Beijing, China, June. ACM Press.

A Hierarchical Neural Network for Information Extraction of Product Attribute and Condition Sentences

Yukinori Homma, Kugatsu Sadamitsu, Kyosuke Nishida,
Ryuichiro Higashinaka, Hisako Asano and Yoshihiro Matsuo
NTT Media Intelligence Laboratories, NTT Corporation
1-1 Hikari-no-oka, Yukosuka, 239-0847, Japan
```
{homma.yukinori, sadamitsu.kugatsu, nishida.kyosuke,
higashinaka.ryuichiro, asano.hisako, matsuo.yoshihiro}
                    @lab.ntt.co.jp
```


Abstract

This paper describes a hierarchical neural network we propose for sentence classification to extract product information from product documents. The network classifies each sentence in a document into attribute and condition classes on the basis of word sequences and sentence sequences in the document. Experimental results showed the method using the proposed network significantly outperformed baseline methods by taking semantic representation of word and sentence sequential data into account. We also evaluated the network with two different product domains (insurance and tourism domains) and found that it was effective for both the domains.

1 Introduction

With the increase in the number of product documents in electronic form, it is becoming increasingly important to build technologies to extract information from these documents. In particular, it is useful to extract information about product attributes (such as *"Insurance Premiums"*) and their values (such as *"$ 0.50 per day"*) from web product documents for many applications such as commodity comparison, product recommendation and question answering systems about products. For instance, to provide a question answering system that compares particular attributes of products, we need to extract the values of common attributes from each product document.

In this study, we tackled the following two problems for extracting information from product documents on the Web. The first and main problem is to classify each sentence into attribute classes and the second one is to distinguish whether or not each sentence includes condition information, which is helpful in subdividing the attribute. Figure 1 shows an example insurance product document and an example of classification results of attribute and condition.

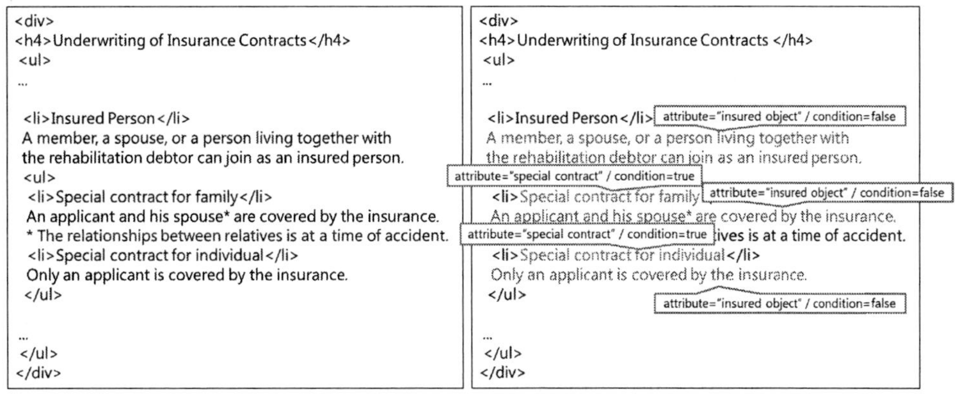

Figure 1: Left: Example of insurance product document. Right: Example of labeled attribute and condition classes.

Proceedings of the Open Knowledge Base and Question Answering (OKBQA) Workshop,
pages 21–29, Osaka, Japan, December 11 2016.

Attribute sentence classification   Product documents in the Web describe product attributes in different ways, e.g. tables, listings and plain sentences. Although most previous studies have tried to extract *words* or *phrases* presenting product attribute values such as *"size"* or *"fee"*, from the above components, we think that it is also useful to extract *sentences* presenting values such as *"overview"* or *"payment terms"* to provide a question answering system that will explain products in the form of sentences. We therefore tackled the following problem in this study.

Problem 1. Given an HTML/XML document, we classify each sentence into pre-defined attribute classes, where a sentence consists of a sequence of words and their tag information.

Condition sentence classification   There are some cases in which common attribute classes are not enough for obtaining concrete information that can be used in question answering systems, and this problem is not able to be simply solved by subdividing the pre-defined classes since the concrete information is product specific. For example, we can see from Figure 1 that there are two special contracts (for family and for individual) that have different values of the attribute *Insured object*. We consider that it is helpful to extract a sentence that presents necessary conditions in each document instead of constructing a detailed taxonomy of product attributes. We therefore focus on extracting sentences describing *condition* information.

Problem 2. We also classify each sentence into condition or non-condition classes.

Given information about the classification results of attribute and condition sentences, we can provide a question answering system which can provide a proper answer based on the terms of conditions. As an example for Figure 1, when a user asks a question about insured objects of the product, such as *"Who is covered by this insurance?"*, and the system understands that the user made *a special contract for an individual*, the system can provide an answer such as *"Since you made a special contract for an individual, the insurance covers only the applicant"*.

To classify each sentence accurately, it is important to consider the semantic meanings of a sequence of sentences and their HTML tag information. For example, sentences in a listing structure will belong to the same class. A sentence also has a sequence of words, and each word has different importance in forming the semantic meanings of the sentence. Recently, recurrent neural networks (RNNs) have been very successful in capturing semantic representations of word and sentence sequential data in several tasks, including machine translation (Bahdanau et al., 2014), Named Entity Recognition (Joshi et al., 2015; Jagannatha and Yu, 2016) and document classification (Yang et al., 2016).

In the work reported in this paper, we attempted to develop a neural network model to capture semantic representations of word and sentence sequential data and classify each sentence in a document into attributes and condition classes. We developed and here propose a hierarchical neural network that classifies each sentence into attribute and condition classes by learning two classification problems jointly. Experimental results demonstrated that our network performed better than baseline methods by capturing the semantics and structures of sentences. We also evaluated the network in experiments with two different product domains (insurance products, tourism products) and found that it is effective for both the domains.

2   Related work

2.1   Word-level attribute extraction

Many researchers have studied the task of extracting values of attributes in a word or a phrase level from product documents. The work they have done can be classified into two approaches: the pattern matching approach based on structured-tag information (Auer et al., 2007; Muslea et al., 1999; Gulhane et al., 2011) and the machine learning approach based on the predefined attribute-values dictionary (Nagy and Farkas, 2012; Jagannatha and Yu, 2016).

The pattern matching approach relies on a set of extraction based on structured-tag information. DBpedia (Auer et al., 2007) is one of the huge structured datasets using hand-made patterns. It extracts structured information from Wikipedia such as infobox templates. Although the hand-made pattern based approach can extract information with high accuracy from documents that have the same document structure such as infobox templates, it takes considerable costs to make patterns to extract information from documents that have a different document structure. Some researchers have proposed methods to acquire patterns automatically on the basis of machine learning (Muslea et al., 1999; Gulhane et al., 2011). Muslea et al. (1999) proposed a method to extract the node path of the DOM tree as patterns. Gulhane et al. (2011) proposed a method to group similar structured pages in a Web site and automatically change patterns to extract information based on the structure of each document. The method to acquire patterns automatically is effective when there are many documents that have similar structures, such as online shopping site documents. However, it is difficult to extract patterns with high accuracy from web product documents that describe product attributes in different ways.

The machine learning approach has been the one most widely studied during the last decade, and many methods were proposed to extract values of product attributes (Nagy and Farkas, 2012; Jagannatha and Yu, 2016). Nagy and Farkas (2012) proposed a method to extract personal information such as phone number, occupation, and address from search result pages corresponding to personal name queries. Since their method focuses on extraction of a value for each attribute from a document and narrows down a range for finding personal information on the basis of the paragraph title, it is difficult to apply this method for extraction of several values that are scattered in a document. Jagannatha and Yu (2016) proposed a method to extract medical events written by a word or a phrase from unstructured text in electronic health record notes using recurrent neural network frameworks. Their model focuses mainly on word sequence information, which is effective for extracting word or phrase values about attributes in the documents. However, since our aim is to extract sentence-level values of attributes in a web product document, we use HTML tags as features and focus on capturing the importance of words in a sentence to classify the sentence by using the attention architecture.

2.2 Sentence-level attribute extraction

A number of related studies have been performed for extracting sentence values of attributes in several tasks, such as event information extraction (Naughton et al., 2008), extractive summarization (Nishikawa et al., 2015) and emotion classification (Li et al., 2015). Naughton et al. (2008) evaluated the performance of a support vector machine classifier and a language modeling approach for the task of identifying the sentences in a document that describe one or more instances of a specified event type. They use the words of a sentence as features and do not focus on the sentence sequences. Nishikawa et al. (2015) proposed a method for query-oriented extractive summarization to extract information especially from Wikipedia article for a question answering system. This method can extract sentences that present values of product attributes using semi hidden Markov models that capture the semantic meaning of sentence sequences in the document. However, since the method depends on a summarization model and extracts sentences only as a value for each attribute, it cannot extract several values for all attributes and conditions in the documents. In contrast, our method learns to classify each sentence into attribute and condition classes by learning two classification problems jointly and extracts information for attributes and conditions from web documents. These documents are not limited to Wikipedia articles.

Li et al. (2015) proposed a method for sentence-level emotion classification in documents. Their method is based on a factor graph with two layers to model the emotional label dependence in a variable layer and model the sentence context dependence in a factor layer. Their experimental results showed that it is effective for sentence-level emotion classification to use both label and context dependence information. While they did not address the importance of words in a sentence to classify sentences, this paper addresses that topic in reporting on evaluation results. Moreover, our method uses HTML tag information as features to extract structural information of documents and classify each sentence into attribute and condition classes.

3 Proposed network

In our study, we focused on a network that would classify sentences into attribute and condition classes by learning two classification problems jointly.

Assume that a document has L sentences and the i-th sentence contains T_i words and tag information

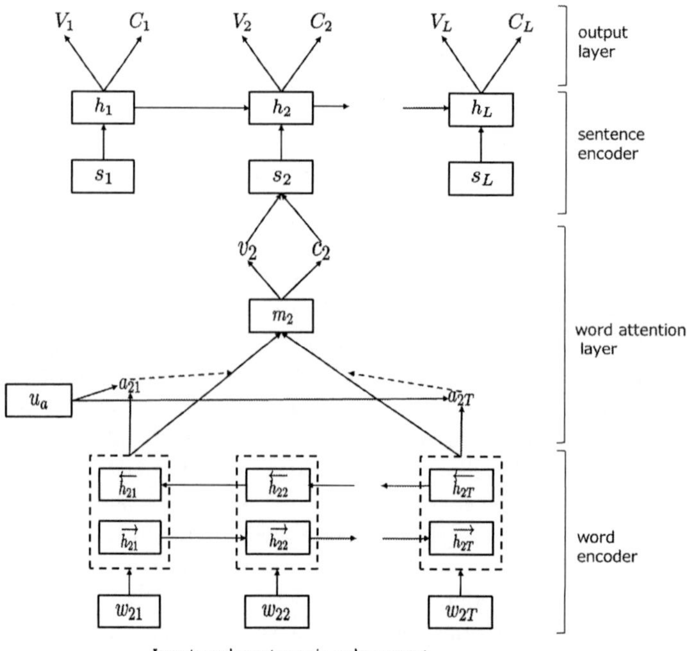

Figure 2: Architecture of proposed network.

t_i. w_{ij} with $j \in [1, T_i]$ represents the word in the i-th sentence. t_i represents the tag name of a parent node of the DOM tree corresponding to the i-th sentence.

3.1 Overview of architecture

The overall architecture of the proposed network is shown in Figure 2. The network contains four components: word encoder, word attention layer, sentence encoder and output layer.

Our network does not learn in an end-to-end manner; we conducted block-wise learning for speeding up the leaning. The learning of the first block of word layers is conducted to obtain a sentence vector, and that of the second block is conducted to classify each sentence into classes. First, it builds a sentence vector that represents the classification probability of attribute classes and condition classes by aggregating important words into hidden sentence vectors m_i in the word encoder (subsection 3.2) and the word attention layer (subsection 3.3) to capture semantic meanings of word sequential data. It then classifies each sentence into pre-defined attribute classes and condition classes (subsection 3.5), taking context sentences into account (subsection 3.4) and using a sentence vector to capture semantic representations of sentence sequential data.

In the following subsections, we will present the details of each component.

3.2 Word encoder

The word encoder builds a word embedding vector for every word in the sentence.

Given a sentence with words w_{ij}, $j \in [1, T_i]$, all words are first encoded into one-hot vectors. A one-hot vector x_{ij} is a binary vector whose elements are all zeros except for the v-th element, which corresponds to the v-th token in a vocabulary V. Then, the one-hot vector x_{ij} is encoded into an E-dimensional vector e_{ij} as the following equation.

$$e_{ij} = W^{wemb} w_{ij} \tag{1}$$

where $W^{wemb} \in \mathcal{R}^{E * |V|}$ is a weight matrix and $|V|$ is the size of the vocabulary.

Next, the network focuses on the context of words in the sentence. Recurrent neural networks (RNNs) with long short-term memory (LSTM) units (Hochreiter and Schmidhuber, 1997) have been successfully applied to a wide range of natural language processing tasks, such as machine translation (Sutskever et al., 2014), language modeling (Zaremba et al., 2014) and so on. However, since standard LSTM networks process sequences in temporal order, they ignore future context. Bi-directional LSTM (BiLSTM) networks introduce a layer where the hidden-to-hidden connections flow in opposite temporal order. These networks are able to exploit information from the past to the future and vice versa.

Our network also has a BiLSTM network architecture. Given an embedded vector sequence $\{e_{i1}, e_{i2}, \cdots, e_{iT}\}$, the network outputs vectors $\{h_{i1}, h_{i2}, \cdots, h_{iT}\}$ as the following equations.

$$\begin{pmatrix} f_j \\ i_j \\ o_j \\ g_j \end{pmatrix} = W^{wh}\tilde{h_{j-1}} + W^{we}e_j + b^{wh} \tag{2}$$

$$c_j = \sigma(f_j) \cdot c_{j-1} + \sigma(i_j) \cdot \tanh(g_j)\tilde{h_j} = \sigma(o_j) \cdot \tanh(c_j) \tag{3}$$

$$\overrightarrow{h_j} = \tilde{h_j}, j \in [1, T] \tag{4}$$

$$\overleftarrow{h_j} = \tilde{h_j}, j \in [T, 1] \tag{5}$$

$$h_j = [\overrightarrow{h_j}, \overleftarrow{h_j}] \tag{6}$$

where $W^{wh} \in \mathcal{R}^{4H*E}, W^{we} \in \mathcal{R}^{4H*H}, b^{wh} \in \mathcal{R}^{4H}$ are weight parameters. The σ and $\tanh$ are respectively a sigmoid function and a hyperbolic tangent function.

3.3 Word attention layer

Recently, attentive neural networks have shown success in several NLP tasks such as machine translation (Bahdanau et al., 2014), image captioning (Xu et al., 2015), speech recognition (Chorowski et al., 2015) and document classification (Yang et al., 2016).

We introduced an attention mechanism (Yang et al., 2016) into the proposed network to extract words that are important to capture the meaning of the sentence. The network outputs the hidden sentence vector m_i in the following equations.

$$u_j = tanh(W^a h_j + b^a) \tag{7}$$

$$a_j = \frac{\exp(u_j^T u_a)}{\sum_j \exp(u_j^T u_a)} \tag{8}$$

$$m_i = \sum_j a_j h_j \tag{9}$$

where $W^a \in \mathcal{R}^{2H*H}, b^a \in \mathcal{R}^{2H}, u_a \in \mathcal{R}^H$ are weight parameters.

The network predicts attribute label v_i and condition label c_i for the sentence, given the hidden sentence vector m_i as input.

$$p(v_i|m_i) = softmax(W^v m_i + b^v) \tag{10}$$

$$p(c_i|m_i) = \sigma(W^c m_i + b^c) \tag{11}$$

where $W^v \in \mathcal{R}^{V*H}, b^v \in \mathcal{R}^H, W^{ci} \in \mathcal{R}^{V*H}, b^c \in \mathcal{R}^H$ are weight parameters.

The cost function L is the negative log-likelihood as the following equation:

$$L = -\sum_i (\log p(\hat{v_i}|m_i) + \log p(\hat{c_i}|m_i)) \tag{12}$$

where $\hat{v_i}$ is the true attribute label and $\hat{c_i}$ is the true condition label for the i-th sentence.

3.4 Sentence encoder

Given a document, the sentence encoder considers a sentence sequence as input to capture semantic representations of sentence sequential data. All sentences are encoded into sentence vectors $\{s_1, s_2, \cdots, s_L\}$.

The network takes a bag of words vector bw_i, one-hot vector of HTML tag t_i and the output vectors of the word attention layer: $p(v_i|m_i)$ and $p(c_i|m_i)$ for the i-th sentence as input.

$$s_i = W^{semb}[bw_i, t_i, p(v_i|m_i), p(c_i|m_i)] + b^{semb} \tag{13}$$

where $W^{semb} \in \mathcal{R}^{(|V|+|V^t|+|v|+|c|)*H}, b^{semb} \in \mathcal{R}^H$ are weight parameters and $|V^t|$ is the size of the HTML tag vocabulary. $|v|$ and $|c|$ are respectively the number of labels for attributes and conditions.

Then, the network outputs vectors $\{h_1, h_2, \cdots, h_L\}$ as the following equations, given a sentence embedded vector sequence $\{s_1, s_2, \cdots, s_L\}$.

$$\begin{pmatrix} f_l \\ i_l \\ o_l \\ g_l \end{pmatrix} = W^{wh}h_{l-1} + W^{we}e_t + b^{wh} \tag{14}$$

$$c_t = \sigma(f_l) \cdot c_{l-1} + \sigma(i_l) \cdot \tanh(g_l) \tag{15}$$

$$h_l = \sigma(o_l) \cdot \tanh(c_l) \tag{16}$$

where $W^{wh} \in \mathcal{R}^{4H*H}, W^{we} \in \mathcal{R}^{4H*H}, b^{wh} \in \mathcal{R}^{4H}$ are weight parameters.

3.5 Output layer

The output layer predicts the attribute label V_i and the condition label C_i in a way similar to that of the word attention layer.

$$p(V_i|h_i) = softmax(W^V h_i + b^V) \tag{17}$$

$$v_s = argmax_{V_i} p(V_i|h_i) \tag{18}$$

$$p(C_i|h_i) = \sigma(W^C h_i + b^C) \tag{19}$$

where $W^V \in \mathcal{R}^{V*H}, b^V \in \mathcal{R}^H, W^C \in \mathcal{R}^{V*H}, b^c \in \mathcal{R}^H$ are weight parameters.

The cost function L is the negative log-likelihood as the following equation:

$$L = -\sum_i (\log p(\hat{v}_i|h_i) + \log p(\hat{c}_i|h_i)) \tag{20}$$

4 Experiments

4.1 Data set

To evaluate the proposed network, we utilized two domain document sets: seven insurance product leaflets (4,695 sentences) and 44 Wikipedia documents (2,655 sentences) about Kamakura, a famous sightseeing place in Japan. All documents are written (in Japanese) in HTML format.

Each sentence in the documents is annotated with labels that represent the value of pre-defined attributes and conditions as determined by an expert. For example, the sentence "Special contract for individual" is labeled as the value of attribute "special contract" and as condition.

We defined 37 attributes for insurance domain, such as "Special contract", "Reasonable cause for payment", " No reasonable cause for payment" and "NIL" and 27 attributes for tourism domain, such as "Overview", "Origin of the name", "Famous product" and "NIL".

4.2 Experimental settings

We evaluated the quality of information extraction by judging whether the extracted values matched the annotated labels, excluding the *"NIL"* label which means that the sentence cannot be represented as pre-defined attributes. We defined the correct values as those for which the annotated labels of the sentence include the extracted values of attributes except the *"NIL"* label. We used a micro-averaged F_1 score as the evaluation metric for the seven insurance domain documents by applying leave-one-out cross-validation and for the 44 tourism domain documents by applying 10 fold cross-validation.

A comparison of our method with other methods follows.

- Baseline MaxEnt: This is a method using a maximum entropy model that selects the $|V|$ most frequent words from the training dataset and uses the count of each word as features. We consider this to be the baseline method for classifying a sentence into value and condition classes using simply words as input features.

- (proposed) HN: This is a method using the hierarchical network described in Section 3. The network captures semantic representations of word- and sentence- sequential data and classifies each sentence in a document into attributes and condition classes.

- HN-word: This is a method using a network that has the same architecture as the proposed network but has no output layer or sentence encoder. The network takes only the word-sequential information as input features to classify a sentence into value and condition classes. We used this method to evaluate the effects of using sentence-sequential information to classify a sentence.

- HN-sent: This is a method using a network that has the same architecture as the proposed network but has no word encoder or word attention layer. The network ignores the word-sequential information and uses the count of each word as features in classifying a sentence into value and condition classes. We used this method to evaluate the effects of using word-sequential information and an attention mechanism to classify a sentence.

4.3 Model parameters

The hyper parameters of the models for the four methods above were tuned experimentally. In our experiments, we set the word embedding dimension E to be 100 and hidden layer dimension H to be 200. The size of the vocabulary for words V and HTML tags V^t respectively are set to be 4000 and 50. We selected words in the vocabulary as V words of the highest frequency in all datasets.

We used Chainer (Tokui et al., 2015), a framework of neural networks, for implementing our architecture. We used Adadelta (Zeiler, 2012) to train all models and a mini-batch size of 32. In total, 20 training epochs were used.

4.4 Results

Table 1 shows micro-averaged precision, recall, and F_1 scores for the test dataset when each method was trained with a train dataset. The F_1 scores seemed to be generally low as classification tasks since we ignored the *"NIL"* label, which accounts for about 60% of the total dataset. These scores were used to evaluate the quality of information extraction.

Method HN, the use of the proposed network, achieved the best F_1 values in both the insurance and tourism domains and performed statistically significantly better than the baseline method MaxEnt in all of the experiments. Except for condition classification results in the tourism domain, methods HN-sent and HN performed significantly better than methods MaxEnt and HN-word. These results shows that sentence-sequential information is effective in classifying sentences into attribute and condition classes.

Table 2 shows some examples classification results for each method. It can be seen that some sentences in a listing structure were classified into the same attribute class *"No reasonable cause for payment"* correctly by methods HN-sent and HN. This is because they capture semantic representation of sentence-sequential data and thus classified sentences in a listing structure that are close in meaning into the same class *"No reasonable cause for payment"*. On the other hand, MaxEnt and HN-word, which

domain	method	Attribute			Condition		
		P	R	F_1	P	R	F_1
insurance	MaxEnt (baseline)	0.504	0.463	0.483	0.227	0.344	0.274
	HN-word	0.537	0.461	0.496**	0.406	0.301	0.346**
	HN-sent	0.592	0.564	0.578**	0.461	0.291	0.357**
	HN	**0.611**	**0.582**	**0.596****,†	**0.455**	**0.328**	**0.381****,†
tourism	MaxEnt (baseline)	0.436	0.293	0.350	0.500	0.382	0.433
	HN-word	0.443	0.320	0.371**	0.652	0.417	0.509*
	HN-sent	0.556	0.438	0.490**	0.650	0.361	0.464
	HN	**0.562**	**0.459**	**0.505****	**0.667**	**0.444**	**0.533****

Table 1: Micro-averaged F_1 scores for test datasets. Asterisks mean there is a significant difference between the F_1 score obtained for the method indicated and the F_1 score obtained for the baseline method. Daggers mean there is a significant difference between the F_1 score obtained for the method and the next largest F_1 score obtained for another method. (*,$\dagger$: $p < .05$, **: $p < .01$)

HTML tag	Sentence	Predicted label				Correct label
		MaxEnt	HN-word	HN-sent	HN	
<h3>	Reason for not paying benefits	NIL	NIL	NIL	NIL	NIL
<h4>	(the primary contract)	NIL	NIL	NIL	NIL	NIL
<li>	State of health differs from that reported.	*No reasonable cause for payment*	*No reasonable cause for payment*	*No reasonable cause for payment*	*No reasonable cause for payment*	*No reasonable cause for payment*
<li>	Hospitalization due to injury caused before indemnity period.	*Reasonable cause for payment*	*Reasonable cause for payment*	*No reasonable cause for payment*	*No reasonable cause for payment*	*No reasonable cause for payment*
<li>	Hospitalization for reasons other than treatment / unnecessary hospitalization.	*Reasonable cause for payment*	*Reasonable cause for payment*	*Reasonable cause for payment*	*No reasonable cause for payment*	*No reasonable cause for payment*
<li>	Check policy summary for details.	NIL	NIL	NIL	NIL	NIL

Table 2: Example classification results for each method

ignore the sentence-sequential information, incorrectly classified such sentences into the attribute class *"Reasonable cause for payment"*. The reason for these results is that the word information for these sentences is not sufficient for classifying the sentences into the correct attribute classes.

5 Conclusion

This paper described a hierarchical neural network for extracting structured data from product descriptions. The network classifies each sentence into attribute and condition classes jointly in two steps on the basis of word sequences and sentence sequences in the document. First, the network obtains sentence semantics by aggregating important words into sentence vectors. Then it classifies each sentence into pre-defined attribute classes and condition classes incorporated with sentence sequences.

Experimental results demonstrated that the method using the proposed network significantly outperformed baseline methods by taking semantic representation of word and sentence sequential data into account. We found that sentence-sequential information was effective in extracting sentence-level values of product attributes from web documents while word information was insufficient for extracting sentence-level values.

To obtain concrete information that can be used in question answering systems, it is helpful to extract relational information between attribute value and condition sentences. Addressing the problems involved in extracting relationships between sentences remains as a subject for our future work.

References

Sören Auer, Christian Bizer, Georgi Kobilarov, Jens Lehmann, and Zachary Ives. 2007. Dbpedia: A nucleus for a web of open data. In *Proceedings of the 6th Int ' l Semantic Web Conference, Busan, Korea.*

Dzmitry Bahdanau, Kyunghyun Cho, and Yoshua Bengio. 2014. Neural machine translation by jointly learning to align and translate. *arXiv preprint arXiv:1409.0473.*

Jan K Chorowski, Dzmitry Bahdanau, Dmitriy Serdyuk, Kyunghyun Cho, and Yoshua Bengio. 2015. Attention-based models for speech recognition. In *Advances in Neural Information Processing Systems*, pages 577–585.

Pankaj Gulhane, Amit Madaan, Rupesh Mehta, Jeyashankher Ramamirtham, Rajeev Rastogi, Sandeep Satpal, Srinivasan H Sengamedu, Ashwin Tengli, and Charu Tiwari. 2011. Web-scale information extraction with vertex. In *Proceedings of the IEEE 27th International Conference on Data Engineering*, pages 1209–1220. IEEE.

Sepp Hochreiter and Jürgen Schmidhuber. 1997. Long short-term memory. *Neural computation*, 9(8):1735–1780.

Abhyuday N Jagannatha and Hong Yu. 2016. Bidirectional rnn for medical event detection in electronic health records. In *Proceedings of the Annual Conference of the North American Chapter of the Association for Computational Linguistics: Human Language Technologies*, pages 473–482.

Mahesh Joshi, Ethan Hart, Mirko Vogel, and Jean-David Ruvini. 2015. Distributed word representations improve ner for e-commerce. In *Proceedings of the Annual Conference of the North American Chapter of the Association for Computational Linguistics: Human Language Technologies*, pages 160–167.

Shoushan Li, Lei Huang, Rong Wang, and Guodong Zhou. 2015. Sentence-level emotion classification with label and context dependence. In *Proceedings of the 53rd Annual Meeting of the Association for Computational Linguistics and the 7th International Joint Conference on Natural Language Processing*, pages 1045–1053.

Ion Muslea, Steve Minton, and Craig Knoblock. 1999. A hierarchical approach to wrapper induction. In *Proceedings of the third annual conference on Autonomous Agents*, pages 190–197. ACM.

István Nagy and Richárd Farkas. 2012. Person attribute extraction from the textual parts of web pages. *Acta Cybern.*, 20(3):419–440.

Martina Naughton, Nicola Stokes, and Joe Carthy. 2008. Investigating statistical techniques for sentence-level event classification. In *Proceedings of the 22nd International Conference on Computational Linguistics-Volume 1*, pages 617–624. Association for Computational Linguistics.

Hitoshi Nishikawa, Kugatsu Sadamitsu, Chiaki Miyazaki, hisako Asano, Toshiro Makino, and Yoshihiro Matsuo. 2015. Query-oriented extractive summarization for the wikipedia articles using document structure. In *Proceedings of the annual meeting of the Association for Natural Language Processing.*

Ilya Sutskever, Oriol Vinyals, and Quoc V Le. 2014. Sequence to sequence learning with neural networks. In *Advances in neural information processing systems*, pages 3104–3112.

Seiya Tokui, Kenta Oono, Shohei Hido, and Justin Clayton. 2015. Chainer: a next-generation open source framework for deep learning. In *Proceedings of Workshop on Machine Learning Systems (LearningSys) in The Twenty-ninth Annual Conference on Neural Information Processing Systems (NIPS).*

Kelvin Xu, Jimmy Ba, Ryan Kiros, Kyunghyun Cho, Aaron Courville, Ruslan Salakhutdinov, Richard S Zemel, and Yoshua Bengio. 2015. Show, attend and tell: Neural image caption generation with visual attention. *arXiv preprint arXiv:1502.03044*, 2(3):5.

Zichao Yang, Diyi Yang, Chris Dyer, Xiaodong He, Alex Smola, and Eduard Hovy. 2016. Hierarchical attention networks for document classification. In *Proceedings of the 2016 Conference of the North American Chapter of the Association for Computational Linguistics: Human Language Technologies.*

Wojciech Zaremba, Ilya Sutskever, and Oriol Vinyals. 2014. Recurrent neural network regularization. *arXiv preprint arXiv:1409.2329.*

Matthew D Zeiler. 2012. Adadelta: an adaptive learning rate method. *arXiv preprint arXiv:1212.5701.*

Combining Lexical and Semantic-based Features
for Answer Sentence Selection

Jing Shi[a], Jiaming Xu[a,*], Yiqun Yao[a], Suncong Zheng[a], Bo Xu[a,b]
[a]Institute of Automation, Chinese Academy of Sciences (CAS). Beijing, China
[b]Center for Excellence in Brain Science and Intelligence Technology, CAS. China
`{shijing2014, jiaming.xu, yaoyiqun2014}@ia.ac.cn`
`{suncong.zheng, xubo}@ia.ac.cn`

Abstract

Question answering is always an attractive and challenging task in natural language processing area. There are some open domain question answering systems, such as IBM Waston, which take the unstructured text data as input, in some ways of humanlike thinking process and a mode of artificial intelligence. At the conference on Natural Language Processing and Chinese Computing (NLPCC) 2016, China Computer Federation hosted a shared task evaluation about Open Domain Question Answering. We achieve the 2nd place at the document-based subtask. In this paper, we present our solution, which consists of feature engineering in lexical and semantic aspects and model training methods. As the result of the evaluation shows, our solution provides a valuable and brief model which could be used in modelling question answering or sentence semantic relevance. We hope our solution would contribute to this vast and significant task with some heuristic thinking.

1 Introduction

Selection-based question answering (QA) is a task in question answering to pick out one or several parts in a context containing an answer to an open-domain question, where the context comprises of one or more sentences. Commonly, a typical pipeline of open-domain question answering systems is composed of three high level major steps: a) question analysis and retrieval of candidate passages; b) ranking and selecting of passages which contain the answer; and optionally c) extracting and verifying the answer (Prager, 2006; Ferrucci, 2012). In this paper, we pay close attention to the answer sentence selection. Being considered as a key subtask of QA, the selection is to identify the answer-bearing sentences from all candidate sentences. The selected sentences should be relevant to and answer the input questions (Wang and Nyberg, 2015). Several corpora have been created for these tasks like TREC-QA , WikiQA (Wang et al., 2007; Yang et al., 2015), allowing researchers to build effective question answering systems (Voorhees and others, 1999; Andreas et al., 2016; Dai et al., 2016; Yih et al., 2014; Yu et al., 2014; Zhang et al., 2016).

The nature of this task is to match not only the words but also the meaning between question and answer sentences. For example, the answer to "Where was James born ?" is more likely to be "He came from New York ." than "James was born in summer." , even though the latter is more similar in the superficial level. Further, the crisis of the task is to find the sentence most closely related to the intention of the question.

There have been many works towards the sentence selection task (Heilman and Smith, 2010; Wang and Nyberg, 2015; Wang and Manning, 2010; Severyn and Moschitti, 2013). Basicly, those models could be divided into two categories: the lexical models and semantic-based models. The relatedness between the question-answer sentence pair measured by lexical models is mostly based on some metrics such as Longest common substring (LCS), Bag-of-Words (BOW) and Word Overlap Ratio as well as

---

*Corresponding author.

Proceedings of the Open Knowledge Base and Question Answering (OKBQA) Workshop,
pages 30–38, Osaka, Japan, December 11 2016.

Table 1: Some samples in the dataset. The identifier "\t" splits each line into 3 parts: the question, the candidate answer and the label, where 0 is incorrect while 1 is the right answer.

蜓蜥属在哪里有分布？ \t 中文名: 殷鳞蜓蜥 \t 0
蜓蜥属在哪里有分布？ \t 俗名别名: \t 0
蜓蜥属在哪里有分布？ \t 英文名: SouthChina forest skink \t 0
蜓蜥属在哪里有分布？ \t 拉丁学名: Sphenomorphus incognitus \t 0
蜓蜥属在哪里有分布？ \t 地理分布: 分布在台湾南部与东部。 \t 1

Table 2: Statistics of the training dataset. Each pair denotes a question-candidate answer pair. Average Pairs is the average number of pairs in one question.One2One means the question only has one answer while One2Many means at least 2 answers.

Questions	Pairs	Average Pairs	One2One	One2Many	Positive pairs	Positive %
8772	181,882	20.73	8,459	313	9,198	5.06

some complex syntactic matching degree. The semantic-based models usually use some neural network framework to obtain the distributed representation between the sentences . However, both the two categories get some disadvantages. The former could just capture the similarity in literal level , losing sight of the deep semantic information and latent correlation; Meanwhile, the semantic-based models often take much time to train and rely heavily on the provided data. When the train dataset is insufficient or there are some unseen works in test phase, the performance is hard to guarantee.

To solve those problems, we present a model that emphasizes the intention analysis of the question through a feature engineering method. The critical part of the model is to build some efficient lexical features integrated with semantic-based methods to measure the relevance between Chinese question and the answering sentences. Our contributions are three-fold:

- We propose a supervised approach by combining lexical and semantic features to solve the sentence selection task in open-domain QA.

- We explore a feature named Intention Analysis Window Feature which can flexibly construct a strong semantic relation between question and answer sentences. The feature is also capable of integrating kinds of external resources, which could reinforce the performance and effectiveness.

- An efficient Topic Word Extraction method is exploited in our model to successfully filter irrelevant information in answer sentence selection process.

Our model is simple, low-cost in computation and commonly adaptive to various questions. As the result of the evaluation completion shows, the full model is highly efficient, outperforming almost all other models except one with external knowledge resources.

2 Corpus and Problem Description

The aim of common sentence selection task is to choose one or more sentences from the candidate lists to answer the question. At the conference on Natural Language Processing and Chinese Computing (NLPCC) 2016, China Computer Federation, along with the Microsoft Research Asia, organized a shared task evaluation about Open Domain Question Answering in Chinese. One question from the provided dataset in this evaluation is as illustrated in Table 1: each question has a sentences list from which to choose the answer or answers and each question alone with one sentence from its list form a question-candidate answer pair. In the training dataset, the label of every pair has been provided: 1 for right answer sentence and 0 for not. Table 2 shows the statistics of the training data. Most of the questions have only one answer and on average each question has 20.73 sentences from which to choose the answer.

Based on the form of sentence pair in the dataset, we could naturally use the sentence relevance within the pair to classify it. By constructing some suitable features, we take each pair as one sample to

Table 3: Some samples to show the entities close to the interrogative word. The bold words are the Interrogative word while the words with underline show the near entities.

Interrogative word	Samples
谁	电视剧《枪花》中的两大"枪花"分别由**谁**扮演？
什么	楚姓主要的来源是**什么**？
多少	型护卫舰可容纳**多少**人？
哪里	许地山早期代表作《缀网劳蛛》在**哪里**发表的？

train a binary classifier through machine learning method. Finally, we use the score of the 0-1 classification result, which is also the possibility of positive label, as the final score to calculate the MRR and MAP result by the official evaluation script.

3 Approachs

In this section, we describe the approach adopted by us in detail. As mentioned above, the whole model is a binary classification problem according to the relevance between question-candidate answer pair. The main content of this section can be summed up in two aspects: features and training. Section 3.1 contains a detailed description of our Intention Analysis Window Feature. Section 3.2 describes an important preprocessing method adaptive to the answer sentence selection task. And Section 3.3 contains the machine learning model and tool we choose to train our model. It should be pointed out that we use the jieba[1] tools for Chinese text segmentation.

3.1 Feature Description

After analyzing the dataset, we get many question-candidate answer pairs. Startring from basic idea, we can take each pair as an independent sample, then construct features from both literal and semantic aspects. However, we find the fact by experiments that it is quite a rude method to take each pair as an isolated sample. Because it just constructs samples independently from each pair, without considering the differences between various questions. In other words, besides the relation between the two sentences, whether a question-candidate answer pair could be positive label should also be considered synthetically under the whole answer lists of this question. As a result, we design our features under the consideration of the contextual environment.

3.1.1 Intention Analysis Window Feature.

Intention Analysis Window Feature (dubbed IAWF) is a method to get the vectorization representation of the relevance between question-candidate answer sentences pair by making full use of the question intention. This method is quite simple and efficient, and universal to kinds of different questions. In our experiments, this method results in an obvious improvement over the performance of our model.

Most often, during the pipeline of conventional QA system, question analysis is an important step. The aim of this step is to analyze and comprehend the intention, and then to assist in subsequent retrieval and answer extraction. Through a careful observation of the dataset, we find there is roughly a rule that entity closer to the interrogative word covers more semantic information to represent the sentence. As some examples illustrated in Table 3, the entities could properly express the key information of the sentences, especially when given the corresponding answer lists of the question.

Based on this observation, we design an algorithm to make fully use of this characteristics. The whole process is showed in Figure 1. To a question sentence q and a candidate answer sentence x, we first get word segmentation with PosTag (Part-Of-Speech Tag) of q and identify the location of the interrogative word. Then we choose the entities, which have a distance of 1,2,3 to the interrogative word. Each distance is bi-directional, and the entity with a distance beyond the range of the sentence will be set as 'None'. Here we refer the entity to the word whose POS (Part-Of-Speech) is noun or verb. In this way, we get three groups of entities, each of the group has two entities and one of them maybe 'None'. To each entity in each group, we calculate its relevance score to every candidate answer sentence *sent*

---

[1]https://github.com/fxsjy/jieba

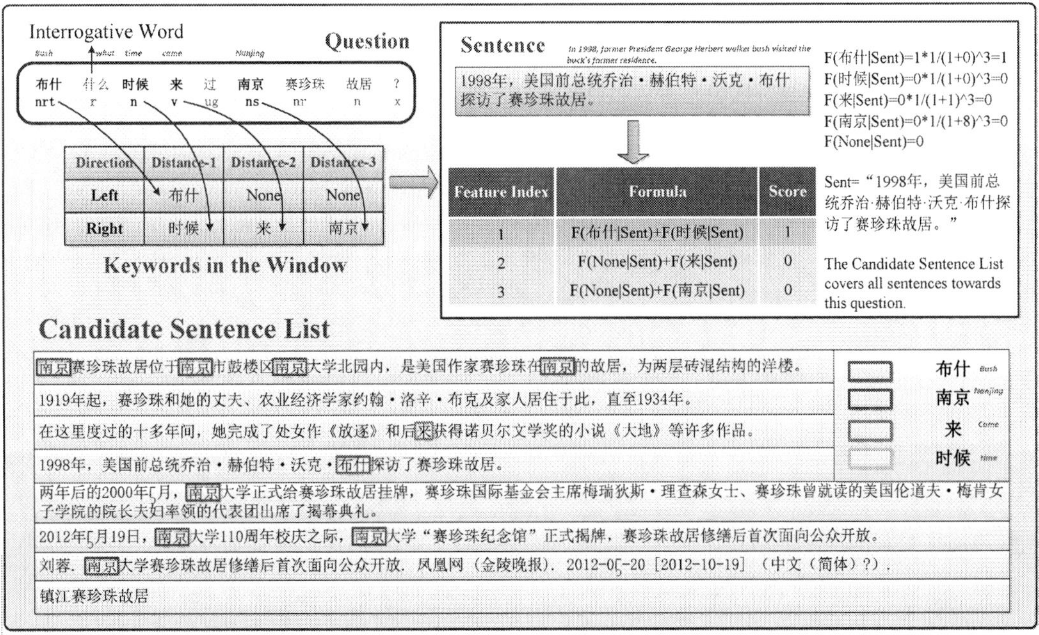

Figure 1: The whole process to extract Intention Analysis Windows Feature with question as "布什什么时候来过南京赛珍珠故居？". The answer list of this question is showed at the bottom. We choose the 4th sentence in the answer list to serve as example. Note that we omit the term of Passage in equation to calculate each score.

according to an idea like tf-idf. To be specific, the score of each *word* to one sentence *sent* in the candidate sentences list *Passage* is:

$$F(word|Sent, Passage) = \begin{cases} \dfrac{\text{sgn}(G(word|Sent))}{\sum\limits_{\{s|s \in Passage, s \neq Sent\}} (1+G(word|s))^3} & else \\ 0 & if \ word =' None' \end{cases}$$

Where, $G(word|s)$ means the times of word appearing in sentence s, $sgn(t)$ is sign function, $sgn(t) = 1$ when $t > 0$ and $sgn(t) = 0$ when $t = 0$.

At last, we add up the score in each groups to get three final score to be served as three features of each question-answer pair.

To summarize, Intention Analysis Window Feature is to choose some entities close to the interrogative word from the question, and then calculate the score of the entities in each candidate answer sentence to measure the relevance degree between the question and answer sentences. If there is an entity from the question has showed only in one of the answer lists, then that sentence should get a high score. If an entity shows everywhere in answer lists, then that entity is mostly an unvalued word.

Of course, the window width of 3 or the index in above equation is not a fixed value. But during the experiments, we find it a suitable choice. Actually, as the average length of the question sentence is within 10, we could easily to lengthen the width of the window to cover more entities in the question sentence even the whole ones. However, the following effect is not good enough. The width of 2 is close to 3, but the width of 4 or more decreases apparently. We think that distant entities bring much more noisy than the beneficial information they cover.

3.1.2 Extension of IAWF

Actually, the basic Intention Analysis Window Feature construct a tight correlation between the question and answer sentences by making fully use of the keyword in the question. However, the critical word from the question sometimes doesn't exist in the answer sentences but be replaced by a highly relevant other word. For instance, for the question " Which season did the ACL 2016 hold? ", the IAWF keyword "season" doesn't appear in answer sentence "ACL 2016 held in summer ."

As a matter of this fact, we make some efforts to extend the IAWF with much more semantic integration. In detail, after getting the important entity , we could freely to import some external resources such as synonyms thesaurus or word2vec (Mikolov and Dean, 2013). The synonym word is the candidate sentence could be roughly considered as the same word of the keyword while the most similar word calculated from the word2vec could also be regarded as a variety of the keyword .Then the equation used in IAWF could be used, with a discount respectively, to get another group of features to model the pair.

In our experiments, the extension of IAWF could handle sorts of questions covering varietal word of the important entity in answer sentence. After extension of the IAWF, the model becomes capable to develop with integration of different resources, result in a wider adaptability.

3.2 Topic Word Extraction

In this part, we describe a very useful trick as a preprocessing method of the dataset. Just like the thought of IDF (Inverse Document Frequency), we find the topic word within the question often has a bad impact on choosing the right answer. For instance, the subject of the question maybe the alias of the topic word about the answer lists, which has showed just once. Then the score of this sentence covering the alias word is very high. However, the subject of the question is usually unvalued to analyze the intension of the question because the whole answer lists are its description.

To tackle this common problem, we manage to extract the topic word off the question sentence by some simple rules. The main rule is to recognize the topic word from the candidate sentences list by some patterns. For example ,the name of one people or place at the beginning of the list usually could be judged as the topic word. This method brings about 3% performance improvement in our test and increase the robustness during the cross validation process.

3.3 Training Model

We have considered some mainstream machine learning model serves as the classifier, including Logistic Regression, SVM (Cortes and Vapnik, 1995), Random Forest (Breiman, 2001), GBM (Friedman, 2001) and XGBoost (Chen and Guestrin, 2016). After referring to some papers (Joachims, 2002; Liu et al., 2016) and doing some simple comparison experiments, we found the XGBoost model almost reached the optimal performance. Furthermore, it is easy to merge with our features processing framework and fast enough. Finally, we choose XGBoost tree model as our classifier. There are some parameters could be adjusted in the XGBoost. Our choice is detailed in the Section 4.

4 Experiments and Evaluation

There are totally 8772 questions in the training dataset of this task, and each of the question-answer pairs has a handcrafted label. To evaluate our model, we divide the 8772 questions after shuffle into training ones and test ones with a ratio of 7:3. And we made 3 pairs of this training-test dataset to evaluate our model with some cross validation method. Besides the Intension Analysis Window Feature, we also build some conventional features to contrast and work together.

4.1 Basic Features

The NLPCC 2016 committee gives 4 baselines result of the train dataset: Average Word Embedding，Word Overlap，Machine Translation and Paraphrase. Further, there are 3 types of features we used in our work.

Verbatim Features. We construct the verbatim features from the literal similarity between question and candidate answer. Simply, we use metrics as follows:

- **Longest common substring.** Longest common substring (LCS) method is a conventional metric widely used in language processing. In this task, we think the length of LCS could reflect the similarity at literal level between the two sentences. Besides, we take the ration of length of LCS to the length of the question as another feature in addition to length of LCS. It could to some extend increase the robustness of this metric.

- **Word overlap.** The same words in question and candidate answer sentence is a clue to find the answer. So we take the times that one word both in two sentences as another metric. Similarly, the ration of word overlap times to total word number in question is also added.

Bag-of-Words Features. Bag-of-Words (BOW) is a common idea in the language model, which is mainly used as a tool of feature generation. After transforming the text into corresponding vector, we can calculate various measures to characterize the text. In our task, the two sentences in each pair could be mixed to form a bag, then the sentences could be vectorized through the bag, making it available to calculate kinds of distance by various mathematical methods. For example, assuming one sentence is " 我\爱\你\大地\母亲\ 。 " while another sentence is "我\爱\你\山川\河流\。 ", then the bag of words will be [我\ 爱\ 你\ 大地\ 母亲\ 。 \ 山川\ 河流]. Following the words order in this bag, the vector of first sentence is [1 1 1 1 1 1 0 0], and the vector of another sentence is [1 1 1 0 0 1 1 1]. The 1 or 0 means the word in words bag is in this sentence or not. Both vector has a dimension of 8, same as the length of the bag. With this method, we construct the vecotors pair according to each question-candidate answer pair. After that, we calculate a series of distance between the two vectors in a pair such as: Cosine distance[2], Jaccard distance[3], Hamming distance[4] and City Block Distance[5]. Each of the results above serves as one dimension in the whole features of a question-answer pair.

Word Embedding Features. It is necessary to consider some suitable features to construct the relevance at semantic level. Naturally, we can use the word embedding trained from large scale corpus to model our sentences. Word2vec (Mikolov and Dean, 2013) vectors, size of 11428967, trained from Baidu baike[6] items are used. Each of the vectors has a dimension of 100. We construct the sentence representation as the average embedding of the words within it. Of course, there are many out of vocabulary words in our task dataset, so we initialize those words to a random 100-dimension vector respectively from Gaussian distribution with mean = 0 and $\sigma = 0.1$. Though the average embedding and random initialization contains some irrationality, for a multiple features engineering problem, each feature can exist a certain amount of imperfection, in the perspective of training it will be automatically measured with a trade-off. After getting the word2vec representation of the question and candidate answer sentences, we use Euclidean, Cosine, Jaccard, Hamming and City Block distances to calculate the similarity. Each of the results above serves as one dimension in the whole features of a question-candidate answer pair.

4.2 Results

The main results of our solution and official baselines are showed in Table 4. We contrast our model with 5 different forms: a) Basic model contains the features from the Verbatim Features, Bag of Words Features and Word Embedding Features. b) IAWF model contains the Intention Analysis Window Features. c) Mix model has the features from both Basic and IAWF models. d) Extension Mix model have the IAWF along with the use of synonyms thesaurus and the features from the basic Model. e) Extraction Mix+Extraction model adds the Topic Word Extraction method based on the Extension Mix model. The features used in each form are simply concatenated to form a full feature vector. It is worthy to know that the dataset of the task is a typical unbalanced one which has too much negative samples than

---

[2] https://en.wikipedia.org/wiki/Cosine_similarity
[3] https://en.wikipedia.org/wiki/Jaccard_index
[4] https://en.wikipedia.org/wiki/Hamming_distance
[5] https://en.wikipedia.org/wiki/Taxicab_geometry
[6] http://baike.baidu.com/

Table 4: The evalutaion results of some baseline method and our soulutions. ACC means the binary classification accuracy.

Model	Method	ACC	MAP	MRR
Baseline Models	Average Word Embedding	–	0.4598	0.4601
	Word Overlap	–	0.5105	0.5123
	Machine Translation	–	0.2408	0.2409
	Paraphrase	–	0.4876	0.4892
Our Models	Basic	0.9475	0.5482	0.5494
	IAWF	0.9616	0.6258	0.6279
	Mix	0.9641	0.7392	0.7409
	Extension Mix	0.9645	0.7652	0.7666
	Extension Mix+Extraction	**0.9654**	**0.7883**	**0.7901**

Table 5: Parameters of the XGBoost tree model.

max_depth	eta	min_child_weight	max_delta_step	Subsample	objective
7	0.06	80	50	1	binary:logsitic

the positive ones. As a result, the classifier tends to predict the negative label because it is easy to get a high classification accuracy. And almost the same accuracy may correspond a big difference in MAP or MRR.

Compared to the Basic model, Intention Analysis Window Features gains a great performance about 10% higher than the ensemble features from Verbatim Features, Bag of Words Features and Word Embedding Features. This demonstrates the effectivity of the Intention Analysis Window Features. Further, the extension of the IAWF brings a obvious promotion of MAP and MRR though the Mix model has already gotten almost 20 features. Besides, the method of Topic Word Extraction promotes the final result and shows a better robustness in cross validation. Finally, training our model with the whole given training dataset, under the best features and parameters, we get the performance of MAP=0.8263 and MRR=0.8269 in the test dataset given by the NLPCC official results.

To be specific about the training model, the final parameters of the XGBoost tree model we used is set as the Table 5. We find that the parameter tuning is an important process to affect the final metric. However, the parameters with a reasonable range are easy to find after a few attempts. Parameters with reasonable range could almost reach limit of the features and plenty of fine tuning could at most affect the MAP or MRR by only 1.5%. That is to say, parameter tuning should not be regarded as the key point of the system and the features themselves are the critical factor.

At the beginning of the process to construct the features, we just do experiments on one training-test dataset and with the same parameters of XGBoost. Because the upside potential of the feature engineering is quite large and far away from the limit. And the best parameters are gained from the result of cross validation at the final phase of the feature engineering.

5 Discussion

From the whole process of construction, adjustment and experiments, we get some intuition and experience within the sentence selection task.

Firstly, the candidate sentences list is crucial to the success of the question. As the promotion of result brought by the IAWF model shows, the isolate basic features couldn't catch the specificity of every candidate sentence list. Only by analyzing the question intension under the environment of context could the purpose be extracted correctly. So, under the consideration of a fine traditional QA system, retrieval of candidate passages or sentences is of much importance before the sentence selection.

Secondly, from the proper functioning of the IAWF models, we can draw a impression that the syntactic construction of the answer sentence has very litter impact on the analysis of the intension. Because the algorithm we use take the answer sentences as a unordered bag rather than a sequence. So we infer with a bit radicalness that the Recurrent Neural Networks (RNN), which focus on sequential information, maybe not a proper choice. As far as we know, the best result of the evaluation solution also choose the framework of Convolutional Neural Network (CNN).

Finally, from feature engineering's point of view, the IAWF gets great progress, more than 10% in specific, after mixing with the basic literal features. This phenomenon means that these two groups of features is highly complementary, completing different functions in this task. Unlike the LCS or Word Overlap features, the IAWF gives much attention about the individual keyword within the QA process rather than the similarity between two whole sentences.

However, there is still much work to do. Our model is still unable to exactly handle some question whose purpose is to choose a subclass of the keywork. And we just test our approach in Chinese QA, other languages also need to be examined to find out whether this method or some conclusion is fit to general language phenomenon or just chinese Characteristics.

6 Conclusion

This paper presents the solution of our model with feature engineering in open-domain document based question answering task at NLPCC 2016 conference. In our model, the combination of some conventional and original, lexical and semantic-based features along with useful extraction method is employed to construct feature groups for the question answering pairs. Our solution can be successfully conducted with a high speed and at very low computation cost. The results show that our model is simple and efficient.

Acknowledgements

We thank the anonymous reviewers for their insightful comments, and this work was supported by the Strategic Priority Research Program of the Chinese Academy of Sciences (Grant No. XD-B02070005), the National High Technology Research and Development Program of China (863 Program) (Grant No. 2015AA015402) and the National Natural Science Foundation (Grant No. 61602479).

References

Jacob Andreas, Marcus Rohrbach, Trevor Darrell, and Dan Klein. 2016. Learning to compose neural networks for question answering. In *NAACL*.

Leo Breiman. 2001. Random forests. *Machine Learning*, 45(1):5–32.

Tianqi Chen and Carlos Guestrin. 2016. Xgboost: A scalable tree boosting system. In *KDD*. ACM.

Corinna Cortes and Vladimir Vapnik. 1995. Support-vector networks. *Machine learning*, 20(3):273–297.

Zihang Dai, Lei Li, and Wei Xu. 2016. Cfo: Conditional focused neural question answering with large-scale knowledge bases. In *ACL*.

David A Ferrucci. 2012. Introduction to this is watson. *Ibm Journal of Research and Development*, 56.

Jerome H Friedman. 2001. Greedy function approximation: a gradient boosting machine. *Annals of statistics*, pages 1189–1232.

Michael Heilman and Noah A Smith. 2010. Tree edit models for recognizing textual entailments, paraphrases, and answers to questions.

Thorsten Joachims. 2002. *Learning to classify text using support vector machines: Methods, theory and algorithms*. Kluwer Academic Publishers.

Guimei Liu, Tam T Nguyen, Gang Zhao, Wei Zha, Jianbo Yang, Jianneng Cao, Min Wu, Peilin Zhao, and Wei Chen. 2016. Repeat buyer prediction for e-commerce. In *KDD*. ACM.

T Mikolov and J Dean. 2013. Distributed representations of words and phrases and their compositionality. *NIPS*.

John M Prager. 2006. Open-domain question: answering. *Foundations and Trends in Information Retrieval*, 1(2):91–231.

Aliaksei Severyn and Alessandro Moschitti. 2013. Automatic feature engineering for answer selection and extraction.

Ellen M Voorhees et al. 1999. The trec-8 question answering track report. In *Trec*, volume 99, pages 77–82.

Mengqiu Wang and Christopher D Manning. 2010. Probabilistic tree-edit models with structured latent variables for textual entailment and question answering.

Di Wang and Eric Nyberg. 2015. A long short-term memory model for answer sentence selection in question answering.

Mengqiu Wang, Noah A Smith, and Teruko Mitamura. 2007. What is the jeopardy model? a quasi-synchronous grammar for qa.

Yi Yang, Wentau Yih, and Christopher Meek. 2015. Wikiqa: A challenge dataset for open-domain question answering.

Wen-tau Yih, Xiaodong He, and Christopher Meek. 2014. Semantic parsing for single-relation question answering. In *ACL*, pages 643–648. Citeseer.

Lei Yu, Karl Moritz Hermann, Phil Blunsom, and Stephen Pulman. 2014. Deep learning for answer sentence selection. *arXiv preprint arXiv:1412.1632*.

Yuanzhe Zhang, Shizhu He, Kang Liu, and Jun Zhao. 2016. Attention mechanism on question answering over knowledge bases. In *AAAI*.

An Entity-Based approach to Answering Recurrent and Non-Recurrent Questions with Past Answers

Anietie Andy
Howard University
anietie.andy@bison.howard.edu

Mugizi Rwebangira
Howard University
rweba@scs.howard.edu

Satoshi Sekine
New York University
sekine@cs.nyu.edu

Abstract

Community question answering (CQA) systems such as Yahoo! Answers allow registered-users to ask and answer questions in various question categories. However, a significant percentage of asked questions in Yahoo! Answers are unanswered. In this paper, we propose to reduce this percentage by reusing answers to past resolved questions from the site. Specifically, we propose to satisfy unanswered questions in entity rich categories by searching for and reusing the best answers to past resolved questions with shared needs. For unanswered questions that do not have a past resolved question with a shared need, we propose to use the best answer to a past resolved question with similar needs. Our experiments on a Yahoo! Answers dataset shows that our approach retrieves most of the past resolved questions that have shared or similar needs to unanswered questions.

1 Introduction

Community question answering (CQA) systems such as Yahoo! Answers are online systems that allow signed-in users to ask, answer, and view questions and answers in a predetermined number of question categories. In Yahoo! Answers, there are two parts to a question: (I) the title - a brief description of the question, and (II) the content - a detailed description of the question (Dror et al., 2011). Despite the active user participation in Yahoo! Answers, a significant percentage of questions remain unanswered (Li and King, 2010). An analysis of Yahoo! Answers data showed that 15% of questions did not receive any answer; however, approximately 25% of questions, at the title-level, in certain Yahoo! Answers categories were recurrent (Shtok et al., 2012), thereby showing the potential of reusing the best answers to past resolved questions to satisfy unanswered questions, with shared needs. Some unanswered questions do not have a past resolved question with a shared need. For example, given the unanswered question *"How can one win a trip to 2006 FIFA World Cup in Germany?"*, the following past resolved question could be recommended, *"How do I buy FIFA 2006 tickets in US?"*. These two questions do not have a shared need but they do have a similar need, namely *"attending the FIFA world cup"*.

In this paper we claim that using cosine similarity with an entity-linking and knowledge base (KB) approach in question categories with high entity usage retrieves most of the past resolved questions with shared or similar needs to unanswered questions. We investigated this claim by labelling a sample dataset of 50 question pairs from the *Sports* and *Entertainment & Music* categories, that exhibited a shared need. We chose these question categories because of the prevalent use of named entities and their variations. Each question pair was associated with a label described below:

Proceedings of the Open Knowledge Base and Question Answering (OKBQA) Workshop,
pages 39–43, Osaka, Japan, December 11 2016.

- *Potential answer*: given a question pair, (Q_{given},[Q_{past}, *Answer*]), *Answer* is a "potential answer" if it can be used to satisfy Q_{given}.
- *Similar question*: Q_{past} is similar to Q_{given} if they both refer to the same topic[1], but the answer to Q_{past} cannot be used to satisfy Q_{given}.
- *Related question:* Q_{past} is related to Q_{given} if it contains a common entity as Q_{given}, but refers to a different topic[1] from Q_{given}.

We used equation 1 below to calculate the entity ratio of the sample question pair dataset.

$$2 * NC/(NQ1 + NQ2) \qquad (1)$$

where, *NQ1* is the number of entities in the unanswered question, *NQ2* is the number of entities in the past resolved question, and *NC* is the number of common entities in both questions. Figure 1 is a plot of the cosine similarity and entity ratio overlap of the sample dataset. It shows that the *potential answer* question pairs have a higher cosine similarity and can be distinguished from *similar* and *related* question pairs. However, *similar* and *related* question pairs are not easily distinguishable. Our proposed algorithm will aim to distinguish between these question pairs.

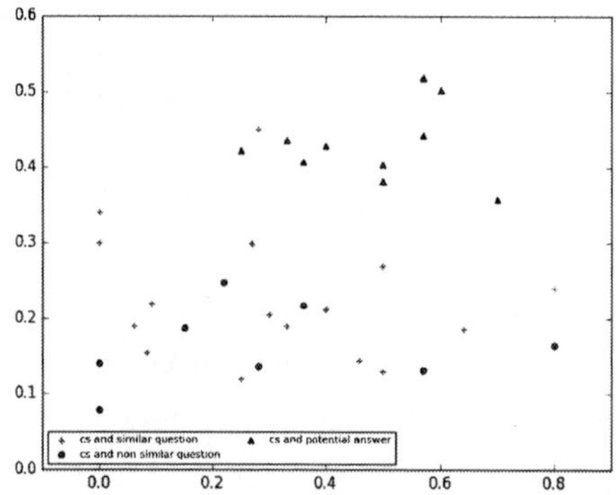

Figure 1: Cosine similarity and number of similar entities in question pair

From this sample dataset, we noticed that the higher the number of common entities or entity variations in a question pair, the easier it is to use cosine similarity to distinguish the question pair categories i.e. *potential answers, similar questions, related questions.* entities in a KB (Guo et al., 2013), from the title and content sections of questions.

The key contribution of this paper is to propose an entity-based algorithm to reduce the number of unanswered questions in entity rich question categories by recommending the best answer to past resolved questions with shared needs to a an unanswered question, if it exists, otherwise recommend past resolved questions with similar needs.

2 Cosine similarity and Entity-based approach

Cosine similarity has been widely used to find similar questions and sentences (Salton and McGill , 1986). However, due to the lack of uniformity in CQA users writing styles (Khalid et al., 2008) and the

---

[1] A topic is an activity or event along with all directly related events and activities. A question is on topic when it discusses events and activities that are directly connected to the topic's seminal event

frequent use of entity name variations in question categories with high entity and entity variation usage, similar questions could have a low cosine similarity. Hence we propose an entity-based algorithm to satisfy unanswered questions by reusing the best answer to past resolved questions with either a shared or similar need to the unanswered questions.

The proposed algorithm has two stages:

2.1 Stage One

In this stage, we select a past resolved question as a candidate similar question to a given question if the "question-title" section of both questions have a cosine similarity greater than a threshold, (0.08) and the "question-title" + "question-content" of both questions contain one or more common entities, entity variations, or KB anchor phrases.

2.2 Stage Two

In stage two, the answer to the candidate past resolved question selected in stage one is assessed as a valid answer to the given question (Shtok et al., 2012). Features are extracted from the unanswered question and past resolved question and we train a classifier that validates whether the best answer to a past resolved question can be used to satisfy an unanswered question.

2.2.1 Features

Entity and KB features: We collect the following entity and KB statistics from the question pair: the number of common entities, the number of commom entity disambiguations, the number of common KB anchor phrases, the number of common words and phrases in the the question pair. These features measure the similarity of the entities and words in the question pair.

Surface level features: We extract the following statistics from the question pair: maximal IDF within all terms in the text, minimal IDF, average IDF. Various IDF statistics over query terms have been found to be correlated to query difficulty in ad-hoc retrieval (Hauff et al., 2008; He and Ounis, 2008). We extract the difference between the word-length of Q_{given} and Q_{past} and the stopword count. These features try to identify the focus, complexity and informativeness of the text (Shtok et al., 2012). We also, extract bigrams and trigrams from the question pair.

Lexical Analysis: We classify words in the question pair into their parts-of-speech and extract the number of matching nouns, verbs, and adjectives, if they exist.

Cosine similarity: Cosine similarity is popularly used to show the similarity between documents (Salton and McGill , 1986). We calculate the cosine similarity of the "question-title" and "question-title" + "question-content" of the question pair.

2.2.2 *Classifier model:*

For learning, we used the Random Forest algorithm with its default parameter settings as implemented by Weka machine learning workbench (Shtok et al., 2012; Jeon et al., 2009) with a 5-fold cross validation.

3 Experiments

3.1 Data Construction and Labeling

The dataset used to train and evaluate our system contains questions pairs, (Q_{given},[Q_{past}, *Answer*]), with labels *potential answers, similar question*, and *related question* , described in *section 1*.

To generate the given question and past resolved question pair, we selected 3000 and 5000 past resolved questions from the *Sports* and *Entertainment & Music* question categories respectively from the language data section of Yahoo labs Webscope^{TM} dataset,and Yahoo! Answers dataset (Chang et al., 2008). Given a question from the selected dataset of past resolved questions, we selected a candidate similar question from the selected dataset if it had a common named entity, entity variation or anchor phrase as the given question and a cosine similarity (> 0.08) . We had three independent reviewers label the question pairs as either a *potential answer*, *similar question*, or *related question*. We selected a question pair if at least two of the reviewers agreed on the question pair label. We calculated the degree of agreement between the reviewers by using Fleiss' kappa [1]. The kappa of our reviewers was *0.448*.

We annotated 400 question pairs from the *Sports* and *Entertainment & Music* question categories and the number of question pairs assigned to each label is as follows: 208 *Potential answers* , 136 *Similar questions*, and 56 *Related question*. We intend to make this dataset available to the research community.

4   Results

We tested two state of the art entity linking tools, AlchemyAPI (Turian, 2013) and Babelfy (Moro et al., 2014) on a sample dataset of questions from the *Sports* and *Entertainment & Music* categories of Yahoo! Answers and AlchemyAPI identified more named entities, entity disambiguations, and KB anchor phrases in the sample dataset. We used AlchemyAPI to extract named entities, named entity disambiguations, and KB anchor phrases from a given question and a past resolved question. AlchemyAPI extracts anchor phrases from the following KBs, dbpedia and freebase.

We carried out experiments using the proposed algorithm on two classes of classifiers, Random Forest and SVM. Table 1 shows that Random Forest performed better than SVM by correctly predicting 87% of the question pair.

Classifier	Percentage of correct predictions
SVM	85%
Random Forest	87%

Table 1: Percentage of correctly predicted question pairs by clasifiers

We also tested the proposed algorithm on *similar* and *related* question pairs. Our aim was to see if our algorithm will distinguish the *similar* questions from the *related* questions. Table 2 shows that the proposed algorithm correctly predicted 77% of the *similar question* pairs. We also tested the proposed algorithm on *potential answer* question pairs and the proposed algorithm predicted 80% of the *potential answer* pairs.

Question Category	Percentage of correct predictions
Potential answers	80%
Similar questions	77%

Table 2: Percentage of correctly predicted potential answers and similar question question pair

5   Conclusion

In this paper, we showed that using cosine similarity and exploiting named entities, entity variations, and KB anchor phrases is effective in searching for past resolved questions in entity rich categories.

---

[1] Fleiss kappa assesses the reliability of the agreement between the raters when assigning labels to the question pairs.

Acknowledgements

This work was supported by the Center for Science of Information (CSoI), an NSF Science and Technology Center, under grant agreement CCF-0939370.

References

Shtok, Anna and Dror, Gideon and Maarek, Yoelle and Szpektor, Idan 2012. *Learning from the past: answering new questions with past answers Proceedings of the 21st international conference on World Wide Web* 759–768

Dror, Gideon and Maarek, Yoelle and Szpektor, Idan 2011. *I want to answer; who has a question?: Yahoo! answers recommender system Proceedings of the 17th ACM SIGKDD international conference on Knowledge discovery and data mining* 1109–1117

Khalid, Mahboob Alam and Jijkoun, Valentin and De Rijke, Maarten 2008. *Advances in Information Retrieval Springer* 705–710

Chang, Ming-Wei and Ratinov, Lev-Arie and Roth, Dan and Srikumar, Vivek 2008. *Importance of Semantic Representation: Dataless Classification* In *proceedings AAAI* 830–835

Salton, Gerard and McGill, Michael J 1986. *Introduction to modern information retrieval* McGraw-Hill, Inc.

Guo, Stephen and Chang, Ming-Wei and Kiciman, Emre 2013. *To Link or Not to Link? A Study on End-to-End Tweet Entity Linking HLT-NAACL* 1020–1030

Jeon, Jiwoon and Croft, W Bruce and Lee, Joon Ho 2009. *The WEKA data mining software: an update* Journal ACM SIGKDD explorations newsletter, 11(1):10–18

Li, Baichuan and King, Irwin 2010. *Routing questions to appropriate answerers in community question answering services.* In *Proceedings of the 19th ACM international conference on Information and knowledge management* 1585–1588

Hauff, Claudia and Hiemstra, Djoerd and de Jong, Franciska 2008. *A survey of pre-retrieval query performance predictors.* In *Proceedings of the 17th ACM conference on Information and knowledge management* 1419–1420

He, Ben and Ounis, Iadh 2004. *Inferring query performance using pre-retrieval predictors.* In *Proceedings of International Symposium on String Processing and Information Retrieval* 43–54

Guo, Stephen and Chang, Ming-Wei and Kiciman, Emre 2013. *To Link or Not to Link? A Study on End-to-End Tweet Entity Linking.* In *Proceedings of HLT-NAACL* 1020–1030

Moro, Andrea and Raganato, Alessandro and Navigli, Roberto 2014. *Entity linking meets word sense disambiguation: a unified approach* Journal Transactions of the Association for Computational Linguistics, 2:231–244

Turian, Joseph 2013. *Using AlchemyAPI for Enterprise-Grade Text Analysis.* Technical report, AlchemyAPI

Answer Presentation in Question Answering over Linked Data using Typed Dependency Subtree Patterns

Rivindu Perera and **Parma Nand**
School of Engineering, Computer and Mathematical Sciences
Auckland University of Technology
Auckland, New Zealand
`{rperera, pnand}@aut.ac.nz`

Abstract

In an era where highly accurate Question Answering (QA) systems are being built using complex Natural Language Processing (NLP) and Information Retrieval (IR) algorithms, presenting the acquired answer to the user akin to a human answer is also crucial. In this paper we present an answer presentation strategy by embedding the answer in a sentence which is developed by incorporating the linguistic structure of the source question extracted through typed dependency parsing. The evaluation using human participants proved that the methodology is human-competitive and can result in linguistically correct sentences for more that 70% of the test dataset acquired from QALD question dataset.

1 Introduction

In this research we focus on generating a sentence which formulates the answer as a natural language sentence and presents it in a more natural form. In particular, if we ask a question to a person, he/she has the ability to answer with a sentence or sentences which has the answer embedded in a context. This form of answering a question is more natural compared to the bare factoid answer delivered by most QA systems.

The rest of the paper is structured as follows. Section 2 discusses the framework that generates the answer sentences. Section 3 explains the experimental framework that evaluates the framework and the results. We also provide a detailed discussion on results in this section. Related work and comparison of our approach to existing work is discussed in Section 4. Section 5 concludes the paper with an overview of the future work.

2 RealText$_{\text{asg}}$ Framework

2.1 Architecture of the framework

We employed the typed dependency parsing (de Marneffe et al., 2014) to determine the linguistic structure of the source question. The core idea in this approach is to identify linguistic patterns based on the typed dependency patterns of source questions and implement answer merging and realization mechanisms for identified patterns. Therefore, new question and answer pairs can be realized to answer sentences using known patterns and by applying associated merging and realization mechanisms. Fig. 1 depicts the schematic representation of the answer sentence generation process. In following sections we first describe the question type identification process and then proceed to a detailed discussion on individual modules of the process.

2.2 Question type identification

Since the answer sentence generation process depends on the question type, it is vital to classify the questions based on the interrogative type before extracting the typed dependency patterns. As the current research concentrates on answer presentation which is the last step of the QA process, we exploited

Proceedings of the Open Knowledge Base and Question Answering (OKBQA) Workshop,
pages 44–48, Osaka, Japan, December 11 2016.

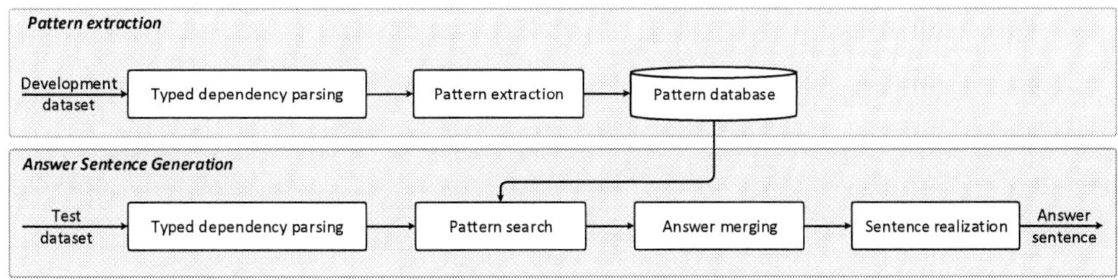

Figure 1: Schematic representation of the answer sentence generation process

both question and the query to classify the questions to the interrogative type. We first classified all questions which require boolean value answers as polar interrogatives. This classification considered both the query and the answer to ascertain that the question is seeking a boolean answer. The rest can be classified as wh-interrogative. However, to further validate this approach, the question text is POS tagged and analysed whether they contain the required POS tags.

It is also important to notice that in this research we do not consider imperative constructs. Imperative constructs are statement which request information such as "Give me information about Steve Jobs". Although such statements still request information from the user, they do not utilize a linguistic structure of a question.

2.3 Dependency tree and pattern extraction

If a sentence (S) is thought as a sequence of words $(w_0...w_n)$ in which the w_0 is considered as the root of the sentence, then a dependency tree is a directed tree originated from the w_0 and has the spanning node set V_S. This tree can also be thought as a well-formed graph $(G(V_S, A))$ in which A corresponds to the arcs $(A \subseteq V \times R \times V)$ created based on a dependency relation set R. Since, w_0 is the root of the tree and dependency tree satisfies the root property (i.e., there does not exist $w_i \in V$ such that $w_i \rightarrow w_0$), w_0 connects the constituents of the tree. Furthermore, if we take a subtree originated from the root, then it can be taken as a phrase given that ordered based on the same subsequence the S is formed of. In essence, the patterns extracted in our approach are first level relations originating from the dependency tree root (w_0). Table 1 depicts some of the syntactic patterns extracted from the dependency tree. We substitute the sub-trees with generic token since their actual words or order of words is not important for patterns except that the relation type originated from the root.

The extracted patterns are preserved as a collection of relations from the root node. In the next section we describe the process of searching for a matching pattern and applying pattern using the specific pattern oriented function.

2.4 Pattern search and application

For each of the extracted pattern in Section 2.3, a specific function is defined with the rule set which defines the order of appearance of the dependency relations in a realized sentence. Once a new question is provided, it is first dependency-parsed and the relations from the root node are extracted. Then the matching pattern is identified and the sub-trees in the question are transformed into phrases associating them with the relation type.

2.5 Answer merging and sentence realization

In wh-interrogatives, answer merging process requires embedding another language segment, however for polar interrogatives this component should target on modifying the polar token based on the answer. The model also embeds measurement units and converts numbers to words. We used the Jena (McBride, 2002) to parse the SPARQL query and identify queried predicate from the SPARQL. The module then searches the queried predicate in a local lexicon database (this is built as a different task in this research (Perera et al., 2015; Perera and Nand, 2015a; Perera and Nand, 2015b)) to identify whether it is associated

Table 1: Syntactic patterns extracted from Typed dependency relations. The pattern is derived from the typed dependencies from the root token. The sign *X* represents a slot which can be replaced with a single or multiple tokens even if there exist typed dependency relations among those multiple tokens. The sign *R* represents the root token of the parse tree.

Type dependency	Extracted pattern

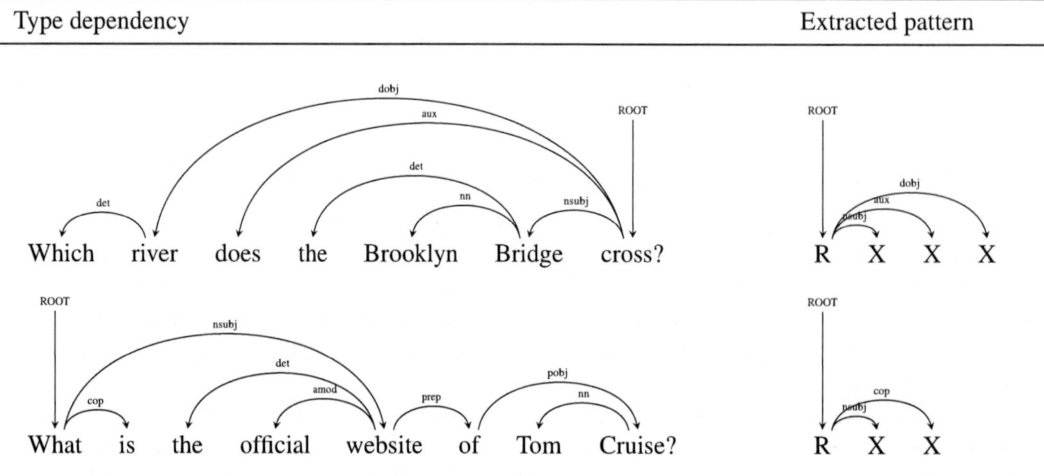


```
PREFIX res: <http://dbpedia.org/resource/>
PREFIX dbo: <http://dbpedia.org/ontology/>
SELECT DISTINCT ?height
WHERE {
res:Claudia_Schiffer dbo:height ?height  .
}
```

⇒ ?height ⇒ dbo:height ⇒ meters(m)

Listing 1: An example scenario of identifying the measurement unit associated with queried predicate by parsing the SPARQL query

with a measurement unit. Listing 1 depicts an example scenario of identifying the measurement unit associated with *height* ontology property of DBpedia.

The sentence realization is based on a linguistic realization module which can further realize the answer sentence. However, by this stage, the answer sentence is nearly built except for the verb inflections. Therefore, this module focuses on realization of periphrastic tense in occasions where the verb can be inflected without compromising the semantics (e.g., does cross ⇒ crosses).

3 Evaluation and results

We were able to identify 18 distinct wh-interrogative patterns and 7 polar interrogative patterns. Using these patterns, answer sentences were generated for the testing dataset with a 78.84% accuracy. Except for 11 questions where the framework completely failed to generate answer sentences, all others were syntactically and semantically accurate. These 11 questions include 5 wh-interrogatives and 6 polar interrogatives. The framework failed to generate answer sentences for these questions mainly due to the absence of rules (for 10 questions) and the errors in the typed dependency parse (for 1 question).

The top-10 patterns were able successfully cover 69.19% of the questions from the testing dataset. Furthermore, the coverage of 51.91% of the questions through top-4 patterns shows that the top patterns are highly representative. We also carried out a human evaluation using three postgraduate students chosen on the basis of having acceptable level of competency in English. The results show that the participants rated the answer sentences with a Cronbach's Alpha values of 0.842 and 0.771 for accuracy and readability respectively. Fig. 2 depicts the weighted average of rating values provided for both accuracy and readability. According to the figure it is clear that the ratings reside between 4 and 5 in the 5-point Likert scale. Furthermore, weighted average rating average for readability is recoded as 5 for 37 cases (90.24% from the test collection) while weighted average rating average for accuracy is recorded as 5 for 31 cases (75.6% from the test collection). This shows that the framework has achieved reasonable readability and accuracy levels from the user perspective.

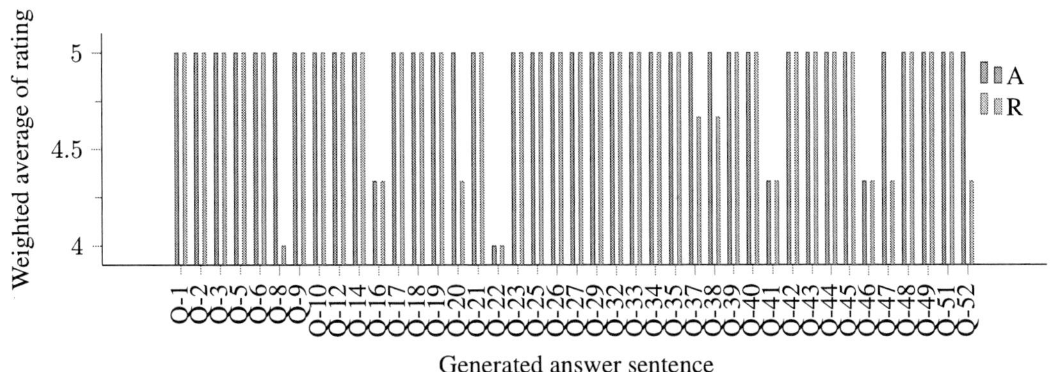

Figure 2: Weighted average ratings provided for generated answer sentences considering both accuracy and readability. (A=Accuracy & R=Redability)

4 Related work

Benamara and Dizier (2003) present the cooperative question answering approach which generates natural language responses for given questions. In essence, a cooperative QA system moves a few steps further from ordinary question answering systems by providing an explanation of the answer, describing if the system is unable to find an answer or by providing links to the user to get more information for the given question.

A successful attempt to move beyond the exact answer presentation with additional information in sentence form is presented by Bosma (2005) utilizing summarization techniques. In this research Bosma (2005) assumes that a QA system has already extracted a sentence that contains the exact answer. He coins the term an "intensive answer" to refer to the answer generated from the system. The process of generating intensive answer is based on summarization using rhetorical structures.

Vargas-Vera and Motta (2004) present an ontology based QA system, AQUA. Although AQUA is primarily aimed at extracting answers from a given ontology, it also contributes to answer presentation by providing an enriched answer. The AQUA system extracts ontology concepts from the entities mentioned in the question and present those concepts in aggregated natural language. However, the benefit that researchers achieved by building the enriching module on top of an ontology is that the related information can be easily acquired using the relations in the ontology.

5 Conclusion and future work

This research presented a novel answer presentation mechanism by generating answer sentences utilizing the typed dependency parse of the source question. The generated answer sentence is further realized using rule a based mechanism to generate more natural sentences. The evaluation of the framework covered how extracted patterns provide coverage in the test dataset as well as the human evaluation for both accuracy and readability. The both evaluations showed that framework is performing well in answer sentence generation by producing sentences which emanate human generated language.

References

Farah Benamara and Patrick Saint Dizier. 2003. Dynamic Generation of Cooperative Natural Language Responses in WEBCOOP. In *9th European Workshop on Natural Language Generation (ENLG-2003) at EACL 2003*, Budapest, Hungary. Association for Computational Linguistics.

Wauter Bosma. 2005. Extending answers using discourse structure. In *Recent Advances in Natural Language Processing*, Borovets, Bulgaria. Association for Computational Linguistics.

Marie-Catherine de Marneffe, Timothy Dozat, Natalia Silveira, Katri Haverinen, Filip Ginter, Joakim Nivre, and Christopher D Manning. 2014. Universal Stanford Dependencies: A cross-linguistic typology. In *9th International Conference on Language Resources and Evaluation (LREC'14)*, pages 4585–4592.

Brian McBride. 2002. Jena: A semantic web toolkit. *IEEE Internet Computing*, 6(6):55–58.

Rivindu Perera and Parma Nand. 2015a. Generating lexicalization patterns for linked open data. In *Second Workshop on Natural Language Processing and Linked Open Data collocated with 10th Recent Advances in Natural Language Processing (RANLP)*, pages 2–5.

Rivindu Perera and Parma Nand. 2015b. A multi-strategy approach for lexicalizing linked open data. In *International Conference on Intelligent Text Processing and Computational Linguistics (CICLing)*, pages 348–363.

Rivindu Perera, Parma Nand, and Gisela Klette. 2015. Realtext-lex: A lexicalization framework for linked open data. In *14th International Semantic Web Conference*.

M Vargas-Vera and E Motta. 2004. AQUAontology-based question answering system. In *Mexican International Conference on Artificial Intelligence*, Mexico City, Mexico. Springer-Verlag.

BioMedLAT Corpus: Annotation of the
Lexical Answer Type for Biomedical Questions

Mariana Neves and Milena Kraus
Hasso-Plattner Institute
August-Bebel-Str. 88
Potsdam, 14482, Germany
`mariana.neves@hpi.de, milena.kraus@hpi.de`

Abstract

Question answering (QA) systems need to provide exact answers for the questions that are posed to the system. However, this can only be achieved through a precise processing of the question. During this procedure, one important step is the detection of the expected type of answer that the system should provide by extracting the headword of the questions and identifying its semantic type. We have annotated the headword and assigned UMLS semantic types to 643 factoid/list questions from the BioASQ training data. We present statistics on the corpus and a preliminary evaluation in baseline experiments. We also discuss the challenges on both the manual annotation and the automatic detection of the headwords and the semantic types. We believe that this is a valuable resource for both training and evaluation of biomedical QA systems. The corpus is available at: `https://github.com/mariananeves/BioMedLAT`.

1 Introduction

Question answering (QA) systems are able of providing exact answers for input questions (Athenikos and Han, 2010; Neves and Leser, 2015). However, coherent answers can only be returned if the system correctly understands the question that is posed. In a QA system, the question processing (or understanding) step includes many components, such as linguistic analysis (e.g., tokenization, part-of-speech tagging, semantic role labeling and parsing), question type identification (e.g., yes/no, factoid, definition), lexical answer type (LAT) identification (e.g., protein or disease name) and query construction.

In this work we focus on the LAT component of a QA system, i.e., the identification of the expected type of the answer that needs to be returned. This is especially important for factoid questions, i.e., questions that expect an exact and short answer in return, such as a protein or disease name. The LAT task can be divided into two steps: (i) recognition of the headword, followed by (ii) its classification into predefined type(s). For instance, in the question *"What hand deformities do patients with Apert syndrome present with?"*, "deformities" is the headword of the question while "Sign or Symptom" is a possible expected type.

Although the field of question answering for biomedicine has evolved in the last years thanks to the many editions of the BioASQ challenges (Tsatsaronis et al., 2015), researchers still miss important resources to support both development and evaluation of biomedical QA systems. BioASQ has provided the community with the most important benchmark in this domain but the dataset does not include information on the expected LAT's. The latter is an important detail, which enables both the evaluation of the LAT identification component in biomedical QA systems as well for training in machine-learning-based methods.

We manually annotated a set of 643 questions from the BioASQ training data with the headword and the corresponding UMLS semantic type. We evaluated our annotations using a baseline approach based on dictionary-based matching of UMLS-derived dictionaries. In this paper, we describe the guidelines

Proceedings of the Open Knowledge Base and Question Answering (OKBQA) Workshop,
pages 49–58, Osaka, Japan, December 11 2016.

and also the results of our annotation process. We evaluate and discuss on the statistics of the annotations, on the complexity of the annotation task and on the error analysis of our baseline approach.

2 Related Work

Construction of a classification of types is common in other domains, such as the PICO framework in the medical domain (Armstrong, 1999). A good overview of taxonomies for the medical QA is provided in (Athenikos and Han, 2010). The UMLS semantic types have also been successfully used for the medical domain, such as in (Kobayashi and Shyu, 2006). During the development of the INDOC question answering system (Sondhi et al., 2007), the authors carried out an analysis of the frequency of the UMLS semantic groups in 106 questions from the OHSUMED collections. The main objective of the analysis was to define different weights for each semantic group in the INDOC system. They report that the most frequent types where the following: "Concepts & Ideas" (CONC), "Disorders" (DISO) and "Procedures" (PROC).

Since the start of the BioASQ challenges, which promoted many innovations in biomedcial QA, some participants have also tried to predict semantic types for factoid questions, as described in details below. However, we are not aware of any previous publications on manual annotation of semantic types and headwords for the BioASQ dataset.

One of the first works to identify the LAT for the BioASQ dataset was carried out in (Weissenborn et al., 2013). Their system classified the question into three classes: (1) What/Which questions, (2) Where-questions, and (3) decision questions. They relied on regular expressions to extract the headword of the question, but they did not attempt to predict the expected types of the answer. They relied on Metamap for mapping the headword to one of the UMLS semantic types (Aronson and Lang, 2010).

In (Yang et al., 2015), the authors extended the work of (Weissenborn et al., 2013) and considered two more classes: "choice" and "quantity". The recognition of the concepts in the question was also performed using Metamap but variants were added with the UMLS Terminology Services (UTS)[1].

The system developed by the Fudan team (Peng et al., 2015) automatically classified the questions into some few semantic types, namely: (1) disease, (2) drug, (3) gene/protein, (4) mutation, (5) number and (6) choice. The sixth type did not indicate a specific semantic type and it was used in situations in which the possible answers are provided in the question, The system used some rules to identify the expected types. The semantic types were also used by the PubTator tool for named-entity recognition. The extracted entities were the candidate exact answers for the question.

The work of (Yenala et al., 2015) was restricted to the identification of the headwords and they developed an algorithm for the so-called "Domain Word Identification". However, they did not attempt to identify the semantic type of the extracted domain words. Instead, the headword is used to filter out words which are not relevant for the passage retrieval step while the extraction of the exact answer was only based on linguistic features and text similarity.

Finally, in the YodaQA system (Baudis and Sediv, 2015), the headword of the question was extracted and its LAT was identified using the titles of the documents in Wikipedia, i.e., by relying on Wikipedia's classes. As an extension of the system to the biomedical domain, they also considered the Gene Ontology (GO) using the GOLR endpoint by considering the type field as the LAT of the question.

3 Corpus Annotation

In this section, we describe our resources, the annotation process and our annotation guidelines for headwords and semantic types.

3.1 Data

We relied on two main resources to perform the annotation of the headwords and the assignment of the semantic types: the BioASQ datasets of questions and the UMLS semantic types.

---

[1] https://uts.nlm.nih.gov/home.html

BioASQ questions. We utilized the questions made available during the first, second and third editions of the BioASQ challenge[2] (Tsatsaronis et al., 2015). The BioASQ challenge includes four types of questions, namely "yes/no", "summary", "factoid" and "list". The "yes/no" question requires either "yes" or "no" answer, while the "summary" question expects a short paragraph as answer. Neither of them require the identification of the semantic type of the answer. Therefore, we carried out manual annotations only for the "factoid" and "list" questions, which expect one or more exact answer(s) of a certain semantic type in return. We downloaded the current BioASQ training dataset[3] in the JSON format and extracted the following information for the "list" and "factoid" questions: (i) question identifier (tag "id"), (ii) question text (tag "body"), and (iii) exact answers (tag "exact_answer").

UMLS semantic types. The UMLS semantic types[4] are a set of categories (and groups of categories) that are used to cluster concepts of the same type in the Metathesaurus (Bodenreider, 2004). It currently contains 133 types divided into 14 groups. We find it is an appropriate resource for the annotation of our corpus given the amount of research that makes use of the UMLS database and the Metamap tool (Aronson and Lang, 2010). For instance, the UMLS semantic types were integrated into the BioTop ontology (Schulz et al., 2009) and previously used for medical QA (Kobayashi and Shyu, 2006). We downloaded the list of semantic types in the plain text format[5] and used it for our annotation.

3.2 Manual Annotation Process

We performed the annotation on the brat annotation tool (Stenetorp et al., 2012). We created the document files by concatenating the text of the question and the exact answers from the BioASQ gold standard (GS) file. We included the exact answer(s) to support the manual assignment of the semantic type (as discussed in the guidelines below). Figure 1 shows an example of an annotated question in brat.

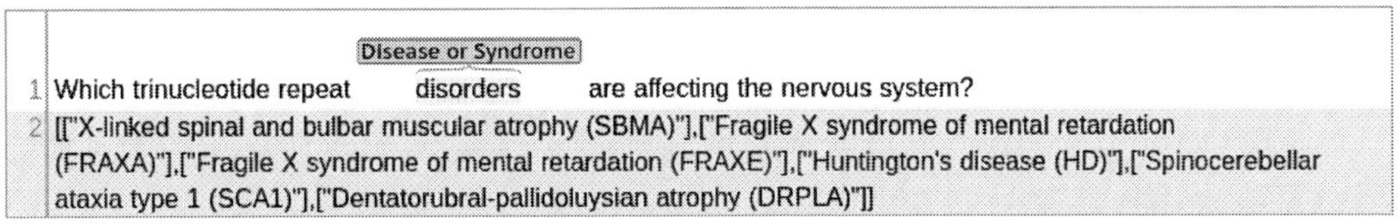

Figure 1: Screen-shot of annotation in brat annotation tool. We included both the question (line 1) and the answers (line 2), just as provided in the BioASQ training set.

Two annotators conducted the manual annotation process: one is a PhD student in computer science who has majored in biotechnology (genetics, biochemistry and bioinformatics) and the other is a computer scientist with deep knowledge and ten years of experience on biomedical natural language processing. Each annotator performed the annotations and then a final version of the corpus was created during many consensus sessions, in which notes were taken on disagreements on both the semantic types and groups.

3.3 Annotation Guidelines

We defined guidelines for the annotation of both the headword of the question and the assignment of its semantic type.

3.3.1 Headwords

We define headword as the minimum text span that identifies the expected LAT. Therefore, it is not limited to the words following the Wh- question word. More details are presented below:

---

[2] http://bioasq.org/
[3] http://participants-area.bioasq.org/Tasks/4b/trainingDataset/
[4] https://semanticnetwork.nlm.nih.gov/
[5] https://metamap.nlm.nih.gov/Docs/SemGroups_2013.txt

1. The text span of the headword should include enough words to support the identification of its semantic type. For instance, in the question "Which are the synonyms of prostate-specific antigen?" (id 5171651e8ed59a060a000009), the headword "synonym" is not meaningful enough to support the assignment of the semantic type, while the phrase "synonyms of prostate-specific antigen" indicates that the answer should be an antigen.

2. The headword should not include unnecessary words that qualify the headword but that have no influence on the decision of the semantic type, such as "of prostate specific" in the previous example. In this case, the headword was restricted to "synonyms of antigens" (discontinuous annotation).

3. In the case of choice questions, multiple headwords were annotated. For instance, the question "Is cancer related to global DNA hypo or hypermethylation?" (id 516e5f10298dcd4e5100007c) has two headwords ("global DNA hypo" and "hypermethylation").

4. Some questions have no explicit headword, i.e, the type of the target is given by the Wh- particle and by the words of the question. For instance, the question "Where is X-ray free electron laser used?" (id 51475d5cd24251bc0500001b) requires a location as answer, given by the "where" particle. However, this particle can lead to different UMLS semantic types depending on the context. For instance, in the question "Where in the cell do we find the protein Cep135?" (id 51596a8ad24251bc0500009e), the answer is a cell component, , i.e., UMLS semantic type "T026". On the other hand, "centromeres" is the answer to the question "Where is the histone variant CENPA preferentially localized?" (id 52fe52702059c6d71c000078), thus, a nucleotide sequence (T086).

3.3.2   Semantic types

We assigned one or more semantic types to the identified headword. More details on the annotation are presented below:

1. The semantic types should be defined not only based on the headword, but also on the exact answers included in the gold standard dataset. For instance, for the question "Which are the best treatment options to treat Helicobacter pylori?" (id 518cb5ab310faafe08000008), the system could return either clinical drugs or procedures as answer. However, given that the gold standard includes only clinical drugs in the exact answer, e.g. "amoxicillin" and "metronidazole", we mapped the headword "treatment" to the clinical drug type.

2. In cases in which the question is composed of more than one sentence, the decision should take into account the complete text and not only the question, as in the following example: "A common problem in proteomics is the contamination of samples with exogenous proteins (often from other species). These proteins can be found in specific databases. List some contaminants." (id 515d7693298dcd4e5100000c). It consists of multiple sentences that are descriptive of the required semantic type. While "contaminants" as headword extracted only from the last phrase would include many possible semantic types, such as the complete group of chemicals or some types of the group organisms, the headword "protein" found in the previous sentences specify the semantic type to be "Amino Acid, Peptide or Protein".

3. We assigned one or multiple semantic types if the answer contained multiple, different types. For example, the answers to "Which substances are dangerous to g6PD deficient individuals?" (id 5314b20bdae131f847000005) are "fava beans" and "primarquine" amongst others. While beans belong to the type "Objects - Food", primarquine can be categorized as "Chemical - Clinical Drug". There were only a couple of such cases.

4   Experiments

In this section, we describe a simple baseline experiment that we performed for evaluation of our corpus. It included both the extraction of the headword and the identification of the LAT. Similar to previous works, we extracted the headword based on both NER and simple heuristics. We used the following regular expression to process a question and to extract its headword: ((what |where |which |who) (<(plural) noun> is| are .*))

After the headword extraction, we performed an NER step on the question. We matched words in the question to UMLS concepts based on various UMLS ontologies. Given the concepts identified in the question, we checked their overlap with the previously identified headword.

For instance, for the question "Which genes have been proposed as potential candidates for gene therapy of heart failure?", we identified "genes" as the headword, using the above regular expression. The same word "genes" also matched the UMLS concept "C0017337" in the NER step. Finally, as the concept "C0017337" is linked to the type "Gene or Genome" (T028), this is the LAT of the question.

5 Results

In this section, we present the details of our corpus and results from our baseline experiments.

5.1 Statistics of the Annotations

The BioASQ training data (cf. 3.1) contains a total of 654 question annotated as "factoid" or "list". We assigned one or more semantic types for a total of 643 questions, as we removed eight BioASQ questions that we found were incorrectly classified as factoid/list (cf. 6.1). We created 647 annotations with a total of 53 distinct semantic types (from 133 UMLS semantic types) and 343 distinct headwords.

Table 1 displays a list of the top eight semantic types that each occurred more than 20 times in our corpus. The number of annotations of these top eight semantic types add up to 406, which corresponds to around 63% of the whole data set. Thus, 45 types account for the other 37% of the annotations.

No. Annotations	Semantic Group	Semantic Type
115 (17.8%)	Chemicals & Drugs	Amino Acid, Peptide, or Protein
72 (11.1%)	Disorders	Disease or Syndrome
62 (9.6%)	Genes & Molecular Sequences	Gene or Genome
40 (6.2%)	Disorders	Sign or Symptom
34 (5.3%)	Chemicals & Drugs	Enzyme
32 (4.9%)	Chemicals & Drugs	Clinical Drug
27 (4.2%)	Physiology	Genetic Function
24 (3.7%)	Genes & Molecular Sequences	Nucleotide Sequence

Table 1: List of the eight top semantic types which occur more than 20 times in the corpus.

Alternatively, QA systems could also consider our annotations only on the level of semantic groups. The 53 annotated semantic types correspond to 11 of the 15 UMLS semantic groups. Table 2 shows the distribution of our annotations over the various semantic groups.

No. Annotations	Semantic Group	No. Annotations	Semantic Group
218	Chemicals & Drugs	24	Phenomena
117	Disorders	21	Anatomy
88	Genes & Molecular Sequences	18	Objects
61	Concepts & Ideas	14	Living Beings
46	Procedures	2	Activities & Behaviors
38	Physiology		

Table 2: List of the eleven semantic groups included in the corpus.

We annotated 343 distinct headwords. The most frequent headwords, i.e., the ones which occur at least ten times in the corpus, are the following: genes (26), proteins (21), protein (19), gene (16), disease (13), How many (11), drugs (10) and diseases (10).

In Table 3, we list the most ambiguous headword, i.e., headwords that can refer to more than one semantic type. This situation was prevalent even for headwords which seem unambiguous at first glance, such as "gene" and "protein". Some headwords, such as "treatment", were ambiguous even with respect to the group, as clinical drugs and therapeutic procedures belong to different semantic groups. This was also the case of the "methods" headword which may also refer to a tool name, thus the semantic type "Manufactured Object".

Headword	Semantic Types
genes	"Gene or Genome", "Classification", "Amino Acid, Peptide, or Protein"
treatment	"Therapeutic or Preventive Procedure", "Clinical Drug"
methods	"Molecular Biology Research Technique", "Research Activity", "Manufactured Object"
drugs	"Clinical Drug", "Chemical"
inhibitors	"Organic Chemical", "Clinical Drug", "Chemical"
mutations	"Genetic Function", "Gene or Genome", "Amino Acid, Peptide, or Protein"
factors	"Amino Acid, Peptide, or Protein", "Disease or Syndrome", "Conceptual Entity"

Table 3: List of some of the ambiguous headwords in the corpus.

On the other hand, very few semantic types were clearly not ambiguous in our corpus, such as the following ones: "Body Location or Region" (headword "region") and "Virus" (headwords "virus" and "viruses"). Although some other semantic types have only one headword in our corpus, these are clearly not the only headwords with which we could refer to the type, but rather that these types are rare in the corpus. Examples of such types are the following: "Group" from "Living Beings" (headword "kingdom"), "Inorganic Chemical" (head word "deficiency") and "Intellectual Product" (headword "articles"). The most ambiguous type is "Amino Acid, Peptide, or Protein" with a total of 55 headwords. Some more examples of very ambiguous semantic types and the corresponding headwords are shown in Table 4.

Semantic Type	Headwords
Cell Component	localization, organelles, cytoplasmic nuclear, structures, subcellular localization, Where in the cell, Where localized
Manufactured Object	software tools, database, databases, bioinformatics tools, biomedical text mining tools, tools, programs, systems, methods, computer programs, content, computational tools
Gene or genome	genes, variant, chromosomes, polymorphisms, orthologs, gene, classes, mutations, genetic determinant, members/isoforms, oncogenes, target, genetic basis, Genes, mutation, gene(s), gene chromosome

Table 4: List of ambiguous semantic types and their respective headwords.

5.2 Evaluation of the Experiments

From a total of 643 questions, our baseline experiment correctly detected the semantic types for 184 (28.6%) questions and the semantic groups for 395 (61.4%) of the questions. The most frequent semantic types that were correctly detected were the following: "Amino Acid, Peptide, or Protein" (58), "Gene or Genome" (T028) and "Disease or Syndrome" (27). These are also the most frequently annotated types in the corpus, as presented in Table 1. Consequently, the most frequent groups correctly detected by our system were the following: "Chemicals & Drugs" (212), "Disorders" (54) and "Concepts & Ideas" (47).

We could not correctly detect many of the semantic types in our corpus. Table 5 summarizes our most frequent errors. All of our top errors are failures to detect the "Amino Acid, Peptide, or Protein" types, given that it contains a variety of headwords. Finally, many semantic groups that we failed to detect were from the very abstract category "Concepts & Ideas".

No. errors	Correct semantic type	Detected semantic type
50	Amino Acid, Peptide, or Protein	Biologically Active Substance
27	Amino Acid, Peptide, or Protein	Quantitative Concept
20	Amino Acid, Peptide, or Protein	Intellectual Product
20	Amino Acid, Peptide, or Protein	Cell Component
19	Amino Acid, Peptide, or Protein	Element, Ion, or Isotope
19	Amino Acid, Peptide, or Protein	Spatial Concept
No. errors	**Correct semantic group**	**Detected semantic group**
116	Concepts & Ideas	Chemicals & Drugs
66	Concepts & Ideas	Disorders
52	Anatomy	Chemicals & Drugs
29	Concepts & Ideas	Procedures
28	Chemicals & Drugs	Concepts & Ideas

Table 5: List of the most frequent errors for the detection of semantic types and groups.

6 Discussion

In this section, we discuss some of the challenges we encountered during the annotation of the questions as well as the results we obtained with our approach.

6.1 Challenges in the Annotation Task

We faced many challenges while manually annotating the headwords and the semantic types in the BioASQ questions. These issues range from questions that might have been mistakenly classified as "factoid" to questions, answers which were too abstract and semantic types which were difficult to identify.

Non-factoid questions. We came across some questions in BioASQ that were probably mistakenly annotated as "factoid" or "list", when they should have been classified as "summary" instead. For instance, the question "Why is lock mass used in Orbitrap measurements?" (id 530b01a6970c65fa6b000008) clearly expects more than one short answer in return, given the "why" particle, and indeed has the following sentence as exact answer:"The lock mass is a compound of known mass and is used to compensate for drifts in instrument calibration." We also found some "yes/no" questions among the list of questions that we analyzed, such as "Is there a crystal structure of the full-length of the flaviviridae NS5(Methyltransferase - RNA depended RNA Polymerase)?" (id 532aad53d6d3ac6a34000010), to which the name of the crystal structure was annotated as answer, though. Furthermore, "Is there a crystal structure of Greek Goat Encephalitis?" (id 532819afd6d3ac6a3400000f), whose answer "No crystal structure of Greek Goat Encephalitis found" is clearly equivalent to a "no" answer. In summary, we removed the following eight questions from our corpus: 54fc4e2e6ea36a810c000003, 530b01a6970c65fa6b000008, 530cf54dab4de4de0c000009, 531b2fc3b166e2b80600003c, 530cf4e0c8a0b4a00c000002, 5348307daeec6fbd07000011, 532819afd6d3ac6a3400000f, 532aad53d6d3ac6a34000010.

Errors in the question formulation. We believe that we found some errors in the question formulation in a way that it leads to wrong semantic types and headwords. For instance, we expected a function as answer to the question "Which hormone receptor function is altered in patients with Donohue syndrome?" (id 2b4/5314bd7ddae131f847000006). However, "insulin", i.e., a hormone, is the answer instead. Therefore, we believe the question should be rephrased to, e.g., "For what hormone is the receptor function altered in patients with Donohue syndrome?". Two other examples of this situation are the following questions: "Which hormone deficiency is implicated in the Costello syndrome?" (id 53130a77e3eabad02100000f) and "Which hormone abnormalities are characteristic to Pendred syndrome?" (id 53148a07dae131f847000002). Curiously, all examples expect a hormone name as answer. In one particular case, we expected a number to be the answer, but the BioASQ gold standard returns a list of cancer types: "How many different subtypes of thyroid cancer exist?" (id 5503145ee9bde69634000022). We did not change the original questions during our annotation.

Challenges on the headwords. For some questions, no headword was explicit and we had to highlight the text span that gave some hints on the headword instead. The question "What is SCENAR therapy used for?" (id 535d69177d100faa09000003) is a good example. It expects disease names as answers and we chose to highlight the discontinuous annotation "what...used for" as headword. A similar example is shown in the question "What does mTOR stands for?" (id 5505a587f73303d458000005), for which we annotated the headword "what...stands for".

Challenging answers QA is a challenging task in itself, but we found questions which were particularly challenging with regard to assigning the semantic type and also for getting the expected answer. For some questions, many other words needed to be taken into account in order to identify the LAT. For instance, the question "What is being measured with an accelerometer in back pain patients" (id 533f9df0c45e133714000016) has the following answers: "Physical activity", "Constant Strain Postures", "Standing time", "Lying time". This is a rather abstract question with answers which do not easily fit any of the UMLS types. We decided to categorize the answers as "Conceptual Entity".

One particular question in the dataset includes two questions with two distinct semantic types: "How many and which are the different isoforms for the ryanodine receptor?" (id 3b1/54db7217c4c6ce8e1d000003). This is indeed a question that a user could ask and the system should preferably provide not only the list of isoforms but also the total number of them. BioASQ provides only the first of the answers but we annotated two headwords ("how many" and "different isoforms") and assigned the two corresponding semantic types, i.e., "Quantitative Concept" and "Chemicals & Drugs-Receptor".

6.2 Agreement on the Annotations

We computed a total of 66 (10.2%) disagreements on the group-level and 49 (7.6%) disagreements on the type-level. This is not surprising, given the challenges discussed above. In general, disagreement on document-level were related to choosing either the "Phenomena" (PHEN) or the "Physiology" (PHYS) groups. Disagreements on the type-level were also frequently related to different types of the "Chemicals & Drugs" (CHEM) and "Genes & Molecular Sequences" (GENE). One example of a divergence on the type can be found in the question "Which are the DNA (cytosine-5-)-methyltransferases inhibitors?" (id 5165932e298dcd4e51000059). One of the annotators assigned the more general "Chemical" types while the other one assigned the "Organic chemical" type. As both types are correct we decided for the more precise annotation "Organic Chemical".

Disagreements on group level also occurred on mistakes of one of the annotators when assigning the "Gene or Genome" (T028) type (group GENE) when a protein (type T116 of group CHEM) was expected. An accurate discrimination of genes, any types of intermediate RNA and the resulting proteins is inherently complex and may be even impossible. This can be exemplified by the question "What are the major classes of retrotransposons active in the human genome?" (id 517843638ed59a060a000036). One annotator assigned the type "Gene or Genome" whereas the term gene can be misleading as retrotransposons can contain no gene-like information (e.g. the Alu element) or multiple genes in one transposon (e.g. LTR retrotransposons). The other annotator assigned a type from the "Classification" group, which is a more general annotation.

6.3 Quality of the Annotations

As discussed above, annotating the headwords and the semantic types is a complex and subjective task. We checked the gold-standard answers from BioASQ upon deciding the semantic types and the two annotators achieved a good agreement score for the group level. However, we neither retrieved nor checked whether the answers have a corresponding concept in UMLS.

Furthermore, most annotations are represented by just a few semantic types. A second iteration of annotation might result in a better distribution of types of the same group. This might be the case especially in the "Disorders" group where most annotations were concentrated on the "Disease or Syndrome" type. Finally, four semantic groups were not annotated in our corpus:"Devices", "Geographic Areas", "Occupations" and "Organizations". Although we might have missed some of these groups during our annotation, our annotations could also serve as feedback for the BioASQ organizers on new topics to address for the next editions of the challenge.

7 Conclusions

We presented our annotation of the BioASQ dataset of biomedical question with respect to headwords and the expected lexical answer types. We manually annotated a set of 643 questions and we provided an overview on the annotations, disagreements and possible mistakes in the questions. We also presented a comprehensive discussion on the challenges that we faced during the annotation process, which could also be translated to challenges to the question answering systems. Finally, we ran baseline experiments to evaluate the extraction of headwords and semantic types.

Acknowledgements

We would like to thanks support from the students Maximilian Götz, Marcel Jankrift, Julian Niedermeier, Toni Stachewicz and Sören Tietböhl.

References

[Armstrong1999] E. C. Armstrong. 1999. The well-built clinical question: the key to finding the best evidence efficiently. *WMJ*, 98(2):25–28.

[Aronson and Lang2010] Alan R Aronson and Franois-Michel Lang. 2010. An overview of metamap: historical perspective and recent advances. *Journal of the American Medical Informatics Association*, 17(3):229–236.

[Athenikos and Han2010] Sofia J. Athenikos and Hyoil Han. 2010. Biomedical question answering: A survey. *Computer Methods and Programs in Biomedicine*, 99(1):1 – 24.

[Baudis and Sediv2015] Petr Baudis and Jan Sediv. 2015. Biomedical question answering using the yodaqa system: Prototype notes. In Linda Cappellato, Nicola Ferro, Gareth J. F. Jones, and Eric SanJuan, editors, *CLEF (Working Notes)*, volume 1391 of *CEUR Workshop Proceedings*. CEUR-WS.org.

[Bodenreider2004] Olivier Bodenreider. 2004. The unified medical language system (umls): integrating biomedical terminology. *Nucleic Acids Res*, 32(Database issue):D267–D270, Jan.

[Kobayashi and Shyu2006] Tetsuya Kobayashi and Chi-Ren Shyu. 2006. Representing clinical questions by semantic type for better classification. *AMIA Annual Symposium Proceedings*, 2006:987–987.

[Neves and Leser2015] Mariana Neves and Ulf Leser. 2015. Question answering for biology. *Methods*, 74:36 – 46.

[Peng et al.2015] Shengwen Peng, Ronghui You, Zhikai Xie, Beichen Wang, Yanchun Zhang, and Shanfeng Zhu. 2015. The fudan participation in the 2015 bioasq challenge: Large-scale biomedical semantic indexing and question answering. In *Working Notes for CLEF 2015 Conference, Sheffield, UK, September 15-18, 2014.*, pages 1337–1347.

[Schulz et al.2009] S. Schulz, Elena Beisswanger, Lszl van den Hoek, Olivier Bodenreider, and Erik van Mulligen. 2009. Alignment of the umls semantic network with biotop: Methodology and assessment. *Bioinformatics*, 25(12), June.

[Sondhi et al.2007] Parikshit Sondhi, Purushottam Raj, V. Vinod Kumar, and Ankush Mittal. 2007. Question processing and clustering in indoc: A biomedical question answering system. *EURASIP J. Bioinformatics Syst. Biol.*, 2007:1:1–1:7, July.

[Stenetorp et al.2012] Pontus Stenetorp, Sampo Pyysalo, Goran Topić, Tomoko Ohta, Sophia Ananiadou, and Jun'ichi Tsujii. 2012. brat: a web-based tool for nlp-assisted text annotation. In *Proceedings of the Demonstrations at the 13th Conference of the European Chapter of the Association for Computational Linguistics*, pages 102–107, Avignon, France, April. Association for Computational Linguistics.

[Tsatsaronis et al.2015] George Tsatsaronis, Georgios Balikas, Prodromos Malakasiotis, Ioannis Partalas, Matthias Zschunke, Michael R Alvers, Dirk Weissenborn, Anastasia Krithara, Sergios Petridis, Dimitris Polychronopoulos, et al. 2015. An overview of the bioasq large-scale biomedical semantic indexing and question answering competition. *BMC bioinformatics*, 16(1):138.

[Weissenborn et al.2013] Dirk Weissenborn, George Tsatsaronis, and Michael Schroeder. 2013. Answering factoid questions in the biomedical domain. In Axel-Cyrille Ngonga Ngomo and George Paliouras, editors, *Proceedings of the first Workshop on Bio-Medical Semantic Indexing and Question Answering, Conference and Labs of the Evaluation Forum 2013 (CLEF 2013)*.

[Yang et al.2015] Zi Yang, Niloy Gupta, Xiangyu Sun, Di Xu, Chi Zhang, , and Eric Nyberg. 2015. Learning to answer biomedical factoid & list questions: Oaqa at bioasq 3b. In *Working Notes for CLEF 2015 Conference, Sheffield, UK, September 15-18, 2014*.

[Yenala et al.2015] Harish Yenala, Avinash Kamineni, Manish Shrivastava, and Manoj Chinnakotla. 2015. Iiith at bioasq challange 2015 task 3b: Bio-medical question answering system. In *Working Notes for CLEF 2015 Conference, Sheffield, UK, September 15-18, 2014*.

Double Topic Shifts in Open Domain Conversations:
Natural Language Interface for a Wikipedia-based Robot Application

Kristiina Jokinen
University of Tartu, Estonia
University of Helsinki, Finland
kristiina.jokinen@helsinki.fi

Graham Wilcock
CDM Interact, Finland
University of Helsinki, Finland
gw@cdminteract.com

Abstract

The paper describes topic shifting in dialogues with a robot that provides information from Wikipedia. The work focuses on a *double topical construction of dialogue coherence* which refers to discourse coherence on two levels: the evolution of dialogue topics via the interaction between the user and the robot system, and the creation of discourse topics via the content of the Wikipedia article itself. The user selects topics that are of interest to her, and the system builds a list of potential topics, anticipated to be the next topic, by the links in the article and by the keywords extracted from the article. The described system deals with Wikipedia articles, but could easily be adapted to other digital information providing systems.

1   Introduction

Smooth human-like interactions to access data in knowledge bases have long been possible with advanced interaction technology. Current applications combine speech and language technology in mobile applications such as Siri, Cortana, and Alexa, to allow chat-like conversations related to topics that are of interest to the user, and the aim is to equip such interactive agents with more knowledge for enabling information exchange with wider topic domains and richer semantics. As argued by McTear et al. (2016), there is a big need for speech-based conversational interfaces that allow easy-to-use, natural, affective, and adaptable interactions with the user, while Jokinen (2009) pointed out that speech makes interactions more human-like and thus increases expectations about the system's competence in natural interaction. One of the bottlenecks for interactive systems has been the amount of data needed for successful interaction management, and usually systems have dealt with limited domains (bus timetables, flight information, pizza ordering, etc.) where the type and amount of knowledge allows the dialogues to be manually structured for the purposes of the task and the intentions of the user.

Robots and virtual agents have made conversational AI agents common and useful for various tasks where interaction with the user is needed. Their human-like appearance calls for more human-like communication, and research has focused on social interaction, multimodal issues, and affective computing for companion applications. Recently, chat systems or non-goal-oriented dialogue systems have also received much attention as they seem to encourage entertaining and engaging interactions as well as provide useful research platforms for studying emotion, social communication, and shared context. For instance, Zhou et al. (2016) describe evaluation of user engagement in a chatbot system, while Otsuka et al. (2016) study responses based on discourse relations.

While earlier work on dialogue systems was based on small, manually structured knowledge bases, we can now take advantage of very large internet-based resources and recent advances in machine learning to train robust interactive information-providing systems. Larger knowledge bases also open up possibilities for systems that are no longer restricted to one particular domain, and enable a move towards

Proceedings of the Open Knowledge Base and Question Answering (OKBQA) Workshop,
pages 59–66, Osaka, Japan, December 11 2016.

open-domain conversational systems which use the knowledge sources to provide chat-type interactions with no dialogue task other than being sufficiently entertaining. However, such open-domain conversational systems are challenging since meaningful interaction also needs to be addressed in terms of dialogue coherence. As argued in Jokinen (2009), conversations are not just a collection of separate questions and suitable answers, but form a conversational thread which exhibits the speaker's intentions of what they want to talk about (topics) as well as coherent and cooperative interaction management. Using the terminology of Grosz and Sidner's (1986) seminal model of discourse structure, dialogue coherence should be formulated in terms of the user's intention, attention, and linguistic processing levels.

Our work has focussed on building an interactive robot agent which converses with the user on the basis of the information found on internet web pages. The WikiTalk application (Wilcock, 2012; Jokinen and Wilcock, 2014) looks at conversational activity from the point of view of constructing a shared context in which the interlocutors exchange messages about interesting topics. The interlocutors' activities concern their reaction to the partner's presentation of new information, and various conversational management strategies which aim to catch the partner's attention, to build mutual understanding, and to keep the flow of information going. We hypothesise that this can be best done via a *double topical construction of dialogue coherence* which refers to discourse coherence taken into consideration on two levels; the evolution of dialogue topic via the interaction between the user and the robot system, and the creation of discourse topics via the content of the digital information article itself.

In this paper, we investigate mechanisms for topic introduction in conversational interactions with a humanoid robot, and discuss models for the computational management of the use of the web as the source of information through which a robotic agent can draw its "knowledge" for the interactions. The work extends open-domain dialogue management towards creating dialogues from any web content, but it also focusses the system on a particular goal in the same way as task-oriented dialogues: here the goal is to provide useful information based on existing web content and to help users to navigate and find the most interesting web pages with topics relevant to their individual interests. The paper is structured as follows. We discuss background for our work and present the problem in Section 2, then continue with the system overview in Section 3, discussion in Section 4, and finally conclude in Section 5.

2   Wikipedia and dialogue topics

In dialogue system design, one of the important issues is to equip the system with appropriate and sufficient domain information. This determines the type of questions the user can ask and the details of information that the system can talk about. The information needed for dialogue systems often already exists in some form, usually as a website, and the question is how to use this information for creating dialogues. In this paper, the first steps are described for transforming information automatically from websites into a natural language dialogue which can be used in building a robot dialogue system.

The focus is on how to present information in a manner that allows the user to follow the presentation and allows the system to anticipate the questions that the user may ask. It is important to notice that although our goal is to build an open-domain spoken dialogue system, we do not aim at a QA-type system that answers questions but rather at a chat-type dialogue system that can follow the user's topic shifts. Open-domain QA systems, such as IBM's Watson (Ferrucci, 2012), use sophisticated machine-learning techniques, question classifiers, search engines, ontologies, summarization, and answer extraction to enable efficient and accurate responses, but the aim of the system is still to find the correct answer to the question, not to hold a conversation about the topic as such. Interaction development has brought QA systems closer to dialogue systems, e.g. the RITEL system (Rosset et al., 2006) has a QA component which is used to ask clarification questions. However, QA systems are still intended to function primarily as interactive interfaces to information retrieval tasks rather than as conversational companions (see Moriceau et al. (2009) for an overview of information retrieval and automatic summarization systems).

In the WikiTalk application (Jokinen and Wilcock, 2014) the user can have a dialogue with the robot in which the robot talks fluently about an unlimited range of topics using information from Wikipedia. The system does not have typical task goals (book a hotel, get timetable information etc.), and is not a typical QA system that provides answers to particular questions. Rather, it aims to function on a more general conversational level and achieve the goal of "provide information on interesting topics" (as long as the user is interested in hearing about it, or the user can switch to a new interesting topic). It is thus important that the system can anticipate what the possible interesting continuations of the current topic are, i.e. what kind of topical interests the Wikipedia article may bring forward. Related topics that the user may wish to continue the dialogue with are marked in Wikipedia with hyperlinks to other entries, so anticipated smooth topic shifts in conversations can be made to the relevant topics via the links.

Following the WikiTalk model, the user can query Wikipedia via the robot and have information from chosen articles read out by the robot. Wikipedia articles are considered as possible topics that the robot can talk about, while each link in an article is treated as new information that the user can shift their attention to, and ask for more information about. The paragraphs in the article are regarded as pieces of information that structure the main topic into subtopics, and they form the minimal units for presentation, i.e. a paragraph can be presented in one 'utterance' by the robot. A humanoid robot with movable arms and legs can also add non-verbal cues to enhance comprehension and to help the user to recognise the discourse level organisation of the text. We experimented with various gestures to provide structuring for the robot presentation, e.g. the robot uses gestures to emphasise the links while reading the text without recourse to explicit link menus, changes posture to mark turn-taking, and pauses after each paragraph to elicit feedback from the user whether to continue on the current topic or not.

In a spoken application, the anticipation of the topics that the user may want to know more about is important in order to assist the speech recognition component to arrive at the correct topical word. The existing method is simply to collect the links of the Wikipedia article and use these as the list of anticipated topics. Coherence of the interaction is thus based on the existing structure of the article and the links between the articles: they form the *first topical construction of dialogue coherence*.

However, the Wikipedia articles may also contain topics which are not currently linked to any other Wikipedia article, i.e. the wikification (Milne and Witten, 2008) of the author's text has not included these concepts in the set of linked concepts, or the article itself brings into the mind of the user topics which are triggered on the basis of the text but are not in the list of links. Our work in this paper addresses exactly this problem: how to anticipate suitable topics for the human-robot interaction when the topics are not explicitly marked in the wikification of the Wikipedia articles. Moreover, if the robot system also needs to relate to other digital resources than Wikipedia, e.g. digital news repositories or other webpages, then a more general anticipation method is necessary, since these resources may not have Wikipedia-type links available for smooth topic shift anticipation. The keyword extraction method to be described below is an alternative method to identify topics and forms the *second topical construction of dialogue coherence*. We call the two processes *double topical construction of dialogue coherence* as it includes two different but inter-related sets of topics to be created and managed by the system.

3   Topic anticipation

3.1   System overview

The WikiTalk system overview is given in Figure 1. The interaction with the user is handled by Conversation Manager which uses dialogue state representations to describe the current state of the conversation, and executes domain-independent dialogue tasks such as informing, requesting more information, clarifying speech input, and giving feedback.

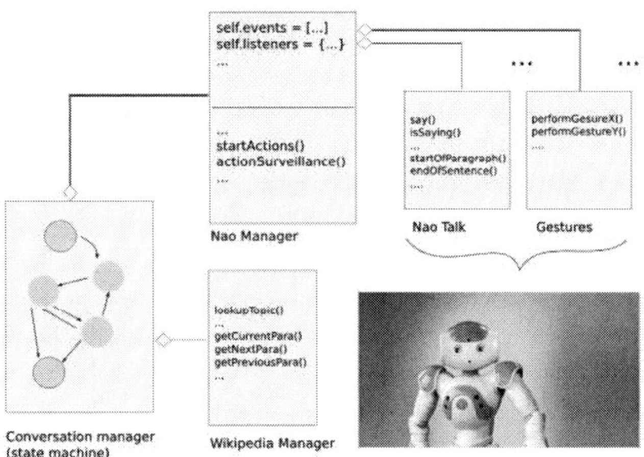

Figure 1 System overview (from Jokinen and Wilcock, 2014).

Conversation Manager receives possible topics and information about Wikipedia pages from Wikipedia Manager which takes care of the Wikipedia interface. The Nao Manager (called so because the robot platform is the Nao robot from Aldebaran) then renders the request via speech and gesture acts.

The domain-specific knowledge is provided through a topic tree (Jokinen et al., 1998; see Section 4), which suggests smooth topic shifts for the conversation. A topic tree is a structure built on the domain knowledge contained in the Wikipedia article. Domain-specific topics are represented by the keywords which describe the content of the topical article, and they form sub-nodes of the current topic node.

The system thus receives two types of possible topics: the links provided in the Wikipedia article itself as well as the keywords produced on the basis of the domain knowledge. Coherence of interaction management can thus rely on the new information provided either by the logic of the wikification of the concepts in the topical article, or by the information content of the article represented by keywords. In this manner interaction management is extended to cover various types of open-domain topics that Wikipedia gives rise to, automatically and without manual annotation, and the interaction between the robot and the user can be made topically richer and more natural.

3.2 Topic anticipation

The topic tree is built by the *Topic Anticipation module* which is part of Wikipedia Manager. It selects the keywords from the Wikipedia article using standard keyword extraction techniques. Figure 2 presents an overview of the system following Jokinen and Mikulas (2016), where the algorithm is described in more detail.

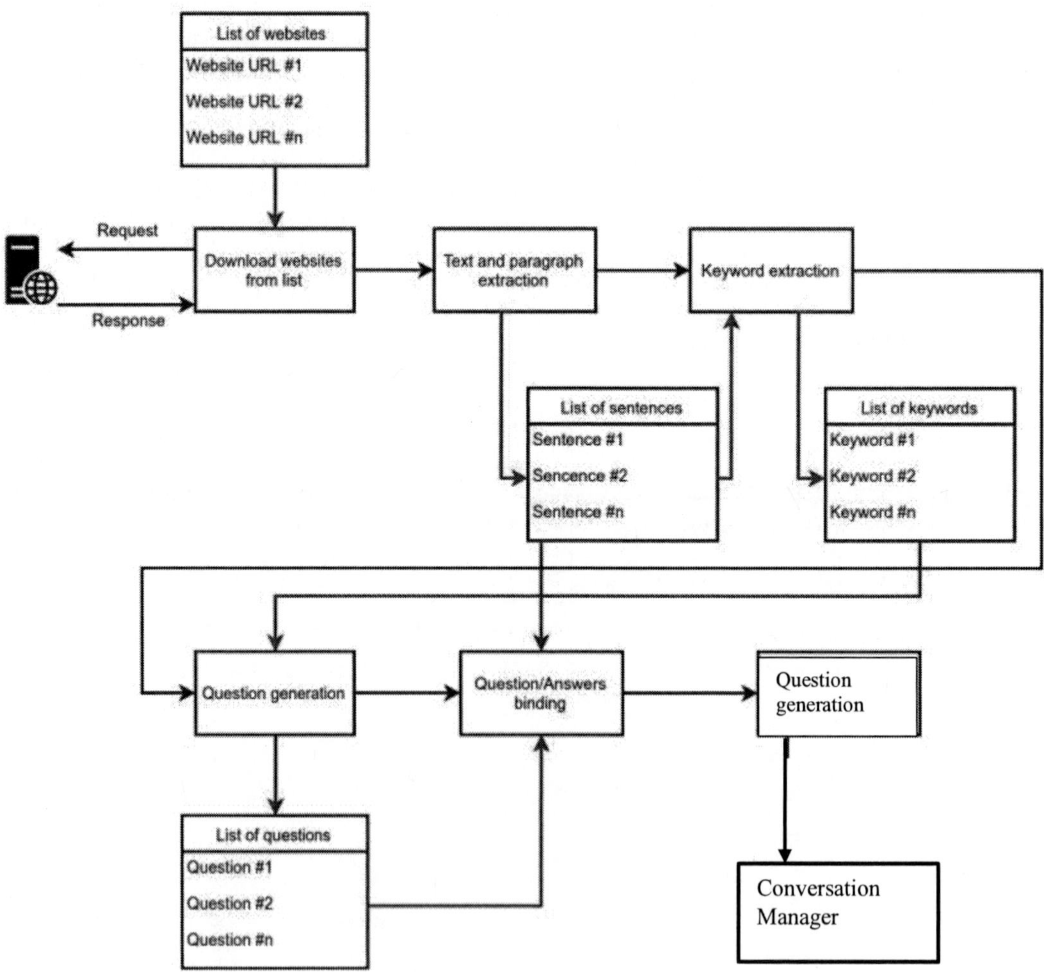

Figure 2 An overview of the topic anticipation module (following Jokinen and Mikulas 2016).

The algorithm first selects relevant sections from the web pages, then extracts text paragraphs from the sections, and cleans up the text before keyword extraction. The extracted keywords are used in question generation, i.e. suitable questions are generated based on the keywords.

Given a webpage like that in Figure 3 about Shakespeare, keywords are extracted from the paragraphs, and they represent a simple estimation of the page content. The keywords are determined via a Naïve Bayesian Filter, following Mooney (2005) and Matsuoka (2003). The frequency calculations currently use text corpora from Project Gutenberg, but we also plan to use larger corpora such as British National Corpus and Google Book Ngram Corpus (Lin et al. 2012) to get more balanced scores with respect to the text genre. The ratio f_p/f_s i.e. relative frequency of a word in the sample data (f_s) and in each extracted paragraph (f_p) measures how frequently a word occurs in the paragraph relative to the normal sample. The best n words are selected as keywords and in our experiments, the value 4 seems to provide the best balance between accurate content representations while also being small enough a number for question generation. By varying n, it is possible to experiment with a small vs. large number of possible keywords, i.e. vary the range of possible topics available for a conversation. In order to optimise the results for dialogue interactions, pruning may be necessary to select appropriate alternatives that accord with the users' preferred questions, or machine learning may be used to learn the user preferences.

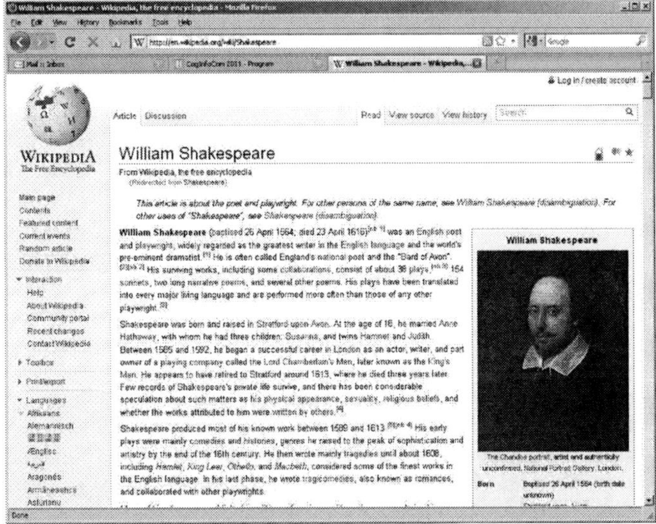

Figure 3 Wikipedia article about Shakespeare.

Some of the keywords extracted from the Wikipedia webpage about Shakespeare in Figure 3 are 'Stratford', 'Hathaway', 'London', 'tragedies', 'Macbeth', 'comedies', and 'romances', which are plausible next topics: places of residence, wife's name, and drama genres. Their scores are:

Stratford	2274900.0	Macbeth	1137450.0
Hathaway	1137450.0	romances	1137450.0
London	1137450.0	later	18957.5
tragedies	1137450.0	death	7109.1

In addition to anticipating the next topics in the conversation, the system's interaction strategies include anticipation of possible user questions to which appropriate answers should be provided. The extracted keywords can thus be used for generating questions which are expected to match the user's interest and include possible next topics that the user can request information about. For instance, in the above Shakespeare example, if the user wants to continue this topic, it is likely that she would like to know more about Stratford or Hathaway or Shakespeare's plays. The keywords thus function as links to Wikipedia articles which are suitable answers to such questions, either because of a direct match with an article title or via keywords related to the article content. The system described by Jokinen and Mikulas (2016) also has a list of template questions which can be used to produce questions by replacing the placeholder with a keyword. A template *Tell me about X* would thus generate requests like *Tell me about Stratford* or *Tell me about Macbeth*. The templates can be used to help speech recognition to recognize anticipated topics, and if the user then utters such a request, the system can map the keyword to a relevant website.

3.3   Anticipating user interest in the extracted topics

An important property of a humanoid robot is its situatedness: the robot acts in the same space with the user, and this contributes to the immediate presence of the robot in the situation. Although robot reactions may be slow, this is similar to face-to-face human interactions where the listener can immediately give feedback on the presented information and the speaker can modify the presentation according to the listener's feedback. The speaker's anticipation of the partner's reaction as well as the listener's attendance to the speaker's presentation appear as co-creation of the discourse, and are manifested e.g. in producing feedback in the form of back-channelling and various non-verbal signals. We believe the Topic Anticipation module supports the above view of interaction: it operates both in the perception and generation phase, simultaneously as the robot tells the information to the user and observes their reaction to the presented information.

When developing systems that can talk about interesting topics with the user, a crucial factor is to assess the level of interest of the user. There are two sides to this: first, how to detect whether the partner is interested in the topic or not, and second, what should the system do based on this feedback The detection of the user's interest level belongs to the system's external dialogue interface and includes interpretation of the user's verbal and non-verbal feedback signals such as intonation, laughing, eye-gaze, nodding, and body movements, to assess her engagement in the interaction (see e.g. Jokinen and Wilcock (2012) and references therein). The decision about how to react to the various degrees of user engagement is part of the system's internal dialogue management, and how this is done is discussed e.g. in Jokinen & Wilcock (2014) and references therein. The interest level is specific to a particular topic, and may change in time. The user may show low interest in the current topic itself, but may show greater interest in a piece of new information that is mentioned.

4   Discussion

In dialogue management, topics are usually managed by a stack, which allows a convenient last-in-first-out mechanism to handle topics that have been recently talked about. However, the challenge in managing Wikipedia-based topics is how to convey the Wikipedia structure to the user so that the user can navigate within the new information links *and* refer to the content of the Wikipedia article she may want to know more about.

We use topic trees (cf. McCoy and Cheng 1990) in which topics are structured into a tree that enables more flexible management of the recent topics than a stack. *Topic* refers to the particular issue (Wikipedia article) that the speakers are talking about, and *NewInfo* is the part of the message that is new in the context of the current Topic (the paragraphs as the robot is reading the text, as well as the links in the article, and the extracted keywords).

Earlier research (as far as we know) has not been concerned with this kind of *double topical construction of dialogue coherence*, and we believe the work described in this paper is novel in that it tries to combine two topical structures: the development of human-robot interaction as coherent topic chains created through the interaction, and the recurring sentential topics that make the Wikipedia texts coherent as discourse. The computational management of the two topic structures and their development are taken care of by the two models: the "traditional" dialogue model is based on the user's interest in a particular topic and is responsible for driving the conversation forward with dialogue acts such as Question and Inform, while the discourse level possibility to create new topics through the lexico-referential topical progression is taken care of by the novel Topic Anticipation component performing keyword extraction. The meaningfulness of the whole interaction is thus built by anticipating possible topical questions via the links and via the extracted keywords, and then by the users' actually occurring choices of topics that they find interesting.

The dialogue coherence appears straightforward: we can rely on the link structure of Wikipedia to provide coherence for the dialogue, but also assume that the keyword extraction provides coherence for the possible continuation of the current topic to one of the keywords. It must be noted that Topic trees created by the keywords and from user navigation via links from one Wikipedia page to another provide a different topic structure from the linguistically oriented topic structure formed from the sentences of the Wikipedia texts. For instance, in the above example of the Shakespeare text, the sentential subjects encode the recurrent topic (Shakespeare) of the paragraphs (subtopics) either directly or through lexical reiteration, superordination, meronymy, or co-reference. The point of departure chosen by the article's writer determines the discourse thematic position of these topics, and all other sentential topics are presented as hierarchically subordinate to it (e.g. *surviving works, Stratford-on-Avon, Anne Hathaway, early plays, tragedies*, etc.). The discourse topic in the webpage itself is constructed through the written coherent text, via lexico-referential topical progression, and it is a different process from the human-robot interaction concerning the robot telling the user about interesting topics.

5   Future work and conclusion

The paper has addressed issues related to *double topical construction of dialogue coherence* in the context of WikiTalk, an interactive robot interface to large digital information resources in the internet. The solution uses natural language processing methods to create automatically a list of possible topics for the robot to continue a coherent dialogue, on the basis of the webpage associated with the current topic of the conversation. The purpose of the work is to extend the system's current method, which uses the explicitly marked Wikipedia links to anticipate smooth topic shifts, with a new capability to anticipate topics which are not linked to another webpage, but which may still be interesting to the user based on the theme of the current webpage.

The work provides another viable avenue to integrate natural language interfaces to novel technological devices like robots, and uses the WikiTalk model to allow access to large digital resources in the internet. Compared with smartphones, tablets, smart watches, etc., a conversational robot interface features more *human* language properties which can be expected to make the query interface easier, more acceptable and accessible. For instance, autonomous robots can move and follow the user independently, rather than be carried in one's hand. This allows people who cannot hold or operate a small device in their hands to talk and hear about the topics they are interested in. Moreover, situated interactions enable multimodal communication which not only provides alternative ways to access the data, but encourages holistic communication between the user and the agent.

In many practical applications, new challenges appear for coordinating and managing online information with the help of natural conversation (e.g. teaching, meetings, non-goal-oriented conversations). Interaction with such applications requires dynamic tracking of dialogue topics and the user's focus of attention with respect to their interests and the actual situation. Thus models and techniques for tracking topics and focus of attention are important, and call for multidisciplinary approaches that combine interaction technology, AI-based system development, and communication studies.

Although the agent's communicative capability can become livelier and push natural language technology forward, the algorithms and methods still need further improvement and testing. For instance, the keyword selection could be elaborated and pruning of the keywords for final application be based on machine learning. Future work will also include more extensive evaluation with the robot agent. The current system has only been evaluated with respect to its operation and first impressions by the users, but a more systematic user study is scheduled to be conducted focussing on a system with keywords selected "as is" and keywords pruned for the purposes of interaction. The evaluation of the topic model in a practical application will also enable assessment of the effect of the humanoid robot's appearance on the user's experience and evaluation of the system, and whether the robot is able to capture the user's attention and contribute to their understanding and topic structuring by its own non-verbal signalling.

A demonstration of the robot interaction will be presented at the main conference (Wilcock et al, 2016) to substantiate the sketch of the dialogue interaction presented here.

Acknowledgements

We thank Mikulas Muron for his work on keyword extraction, and financial support from the Estonian Science Foundation project IUT 20-56 and the Academy of Finland grant n°289985.

References

Ferrucci, D.A. 2012. Introduction to "This is Watson". *IBM Journal of Research and Development*, vol. 56 no 3.4, pp. 1:1–1:15.

Foster, M. E. and Petrick, R. P. A. 2016. Separating representation, reasoning, and implementation for interaction management. In: Jokinen, K. and Wilcock, G. (Eds.) *Proceedings of the Seventh International Workshop on Spoken Dialogue System (IWSDS 2016),* Saariselkä, Finland.

Grosz, B.J. and Sidner, C.L. 1986. Attention, intentions, and the structure of discourse. *Computational Linguistics* 12(3): 175-204.

Jokinen, K., Tanaka, H. and Yokoo, A. 1998. Context Management with Topics for Spoken Dialogue Systems. Proceedings of COLING 1998.

Jokinen, K. and Mikulas, M. 2016. Automated Questions for Chat Dialogues with a Student Office Virtual Agent. Proceedings of the Workshop on Chatbots and Conversational Agents (WOCCHAT), 16th International Conference on Intelligent Virtual Agents (IVA 2016), Los Angeles, U.S.A.

Jokinen, K. and Wilcock, G. 2012. Multimodal Signals and Holistic Interaction Structuring. *Proceedings of the 24th International Conference on Computational Linguistics (COLING 2012)*. Mumbai, India.

Jokinen, K. and Wilcock, G. 2014. Multimodal open-domain conversations with the Nao robot. In: Mariani, J., Rosset, S., Garnier-Rizet, M., Devillers, L. (eds.) *Natural Interaction with Robots, Knowbots and Smartphones: Putting Spoken Dialogue Systems into Practice,* pp. 213–224. Springer.

Lin, Y., Michel, J-P., Lieberman Aiden, E., Orwant, J., Brockman, W. and Petrov, S. 2012. Syntactic Annotations for the Google Books Ngram Corpus. *Proceedings of the 50th Annual Meeting of the Association for Computational Linguistics.* Demo Papers, Jeju, Republic of Korea, Vol 2: 169–174.

Matsuoka, Y. 2003. Keywords extraction from single document using words co-occurrence statistical information. University of Tokyo. http://www.worldscientific.com/doi/abs/10.1142/S0218213004001466

McCoy, K. and Cheng, J. 1991. Focus of attention: Constraining what can be said next. In Paris, C.L., Swartout, W.R. and Moore, W.C. (Eds.) *Natural Language Generation in Artificial Intelligence and Computational Linguistics,* pp 103–124. Kluwer Academic Publishers.

McTear, M., Callejas, Z. and Griol, D. 2016. *The Conversational Interface.* Springer.

Milne, D. and Witten, I. H. 2008. Learning to link with Wikipedia. *Proceedings of the 17th ACM Conference on Information and Knowledge Management (CIKM),* pp. 509–518. New York, NY, USA.

Mooney, R.J. 2005. Text Mining with Information Extraction. Multilingualism and Electronic Language Management. University of Texas. http://www.cs.utexas.edu/~ml/papers/discotex-melm-03.pdf

Moriceau, V., San Juan, E., Tannier, A., and Bellot, P. 2009. Overview of the 2009 QA Track: Towards a Common Task for QA, Focused IR and Automatic Summarization Systems. *In Focused Retrieval and Evaluation, 8th International Workshop of the Initiative for the Evaluation of XML Retrieval, INEX 2009.* Brisbane, Australia, pages 355-365. Springer. Lecture Notes in Computer Science (LNCS 6203).

Otsuka, A., Hirano, T., Miyazaki, C., Higashinaka, R., Makino, T. and Matsuo, Y. 2016. Utterance Selection using Discourse Relation Filter for Chat-oriented Dialogue Systems. In: Jokinen, K. and Wilcock, G. (Eds.) *Proceedings of the Seventh International Workshop on Spoken Dialogue System (IWSDS 2016,)* Saariselkä, Finland.

Rosset, S., Galibert, O., Illouz, G. and Max, A. 2006. Integrating spoken dialogue and question answering: The RITEL project. *Proceedings of InterSpeech '06*, Pittsburgh.

Wilcock, G. 2012. WikiTalk: A spoken Wikipedia-based open-domain knowledge access system. *Proceedings of the COLING 2012 Workshop on Question Answering for Complex Domains.* pp. 57–69. Mumbai, India.

Wilcock, G., Jokinen, K., and Yamamoto, S. 2016. What topic do you want to hear about? A bilingual talking robot using English and Japanese Wikipedias. *Proceedings of COLING 2016*, Osaka, Japan.

Yu, Z., Xu, Z., Black, A.W, and Rudnicky, A. 2016. Chatbot evaluation and database expansion via crowdsourcing. In Proceedings of the RE-WOCHAT workshop of LREC, Portoroz, Slovenia.

Filling a Knowledge Graph with a Crowd

GyuHyeon Choi, Sangha Nam, Dongho Choi, and **Key-Sun Choi**
Machine Reading Lab, School of Computing,
Korea Advanced Institute of Science and Technology (KAIST),
Daejeon, Republic of Korea
{wiany11, nam.sangha, zmal0103, kschoi}@kaist.ac.kr

Abstract

Building accurate knowledge graphs is essential for question answering system. We suggest a crowd-to-machine relation extraction system to eventually fill a knowledge graph. To train a relation extraction model, training data first have to be prepared either manually or automatically. A model trained by manually labeled data could show a better performance, however, it is not scalable because another set of training data should be prepared. If a model is trained by automatically collected data the performance could be rather low but the scalability is excellent since automatically collecting training data can be easily done. To expand a knowledge graph, not only do we need a relation extraction model with high accuracy, but also the model is better to be scalable. We suggest a crowd sourcing system with a scalable relation extraction model to fill a knowledge graph.

1 Introduction

Existence of good knowledge graphs is essential for question answering system. Due to inefficiency of manually adding triples to a knowledge graph, researches about extracting triples from raw text have been being conducted. Relation Extraction (RE) is a task to extract relational facts from unstructured text in triple format. For example, the triple (George W. Bush, parent, George H. W. Bush) can be extracted from the sentence "A president of USA George W. Bush is the son of George H. W. Bush." Various approaches have been researched for RE. We are focusing on two different paradigms here.

Fully supervised approaches require sufficiently many handcrafted training data. A triple is labeled to a sentence if the sentence expresses a certain relational fact between two entities. This kind of manually labeled data rarely has noise, however, it is very costly because annotation takes a lot of time and effort from experts. Manually annotated training data are good in quality but limited in quantity. Furthermore, a new training dataset may be needed for another corpus if the corpus has different characteristics (Zhou et al., 2005). Thus, this model is not scalable.

Another type of approaches makes use of seed patterns. Using seed patterns, triples are first extracted with sentences they are extracted from then extracted triples and sentences are used to generate new patterns. By repeating this process, more and more patterns are collected. This kind of approaches can be an alternative solution when manually annotated training data are not available, however, the noise in triples and sentences tends to propagate over iterations (Bunescu and Mooney, 2007; Pantel and Pennacchiotti, 2006). This model is scalable because it can generate data by itself for the next training but the problem is low accuracy of extraction.

We want a knowledge graph to contain only correct triples. Crowd sourcing is the first alternative to validate triples before they are uploaded into a knowledge graph. We want to take one more advantage in this triple validation process; not only for deciding whether to upload triples or not but also for training a relation extraction model. Needless to say, a better relation extraction model improves the efficiency of crowd sourcing; a larger portion of triples fed back by crowds are valid to be uploaded. We propose a crowd sourcing system that utilizes feedback of crowd's for both triple validation and model training.

Proceedings of the Open Knowledge Base and Question Answering (OKBQA) Workshop,
pages 67–71, Osaka, Japan, December 11 2016.

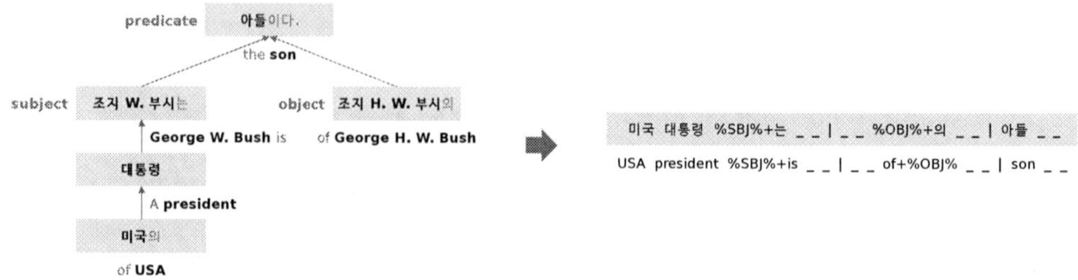

Figure 1: Description of pattern generation from a dependency tree

2 Model Explanation

A model trained by our system consists of patterns and these patterns are extracted from training data; pairs of sentence and triple. To filter out bad patterns, our system uses feedback from a crowd. We will explain how easily a crowd feeds back and our system updates a model later. To maximize efficiency of crowd sourcing, we prefer to get as much feedback as possible per pattern. In other words, we want to have as few patterns as possible. We will also explain the method we used to regulate the number of patterns later in this section. First, we will give a brief explanation about how a pattern is generated in the following subsections.

2.1 Pattern generation

For scalability, our systems uses distantly supervised data to train a relation extraction model (Mintz et al, 2009). Since Distant Supervision uses an existing knowledge graph to collect sentences for training, there is a possibility to gather more sentences as a knowledge graph grows. From a pair of sentence and triple, a pattern can be generated. If named-entities repeatedly appear in a sentence, all possible subject and object pairs are listed first.

Figure 1 describes how a pattern is generated from the sentence "A president of USA George W. Bush is the son of George H. W. Bush." labeled with the subject and object pair (George W. Bush, George H. W. Bush) by Distant Supervision. A pattern is generated using basic Natural Language Processing; dependency parsing and Part Of Speech tagging. In a dependency tree, our system finds the first common predicate which is the first common parent node for both subject and object nodes in a dependency tree. Our system generates a pattern using subject, object, the first predicate node, and their incoming and outgoing nodes. Attributes of pattern are lemmas of the nodes. For nonexistent incoming and outgoing nodes, empty attributes are added to a pattern. Intuition behind this pattern generation is that a key word in a proper position plays an important role to express a relation between subject and object entities. In Figure 1, two consecutive incoming and outgoing nodes are considered.

2.2 Pattern expansion

As mentioned earlier, we want to keep as few patterns as possible for efficient crowd sourcing. It means that our model has to quickly filter out as many bad patterns as possible. To accomplish this goal, Our system uses the special model shown in Figure 2. This model has tree structure and each node has four elements; a pattern, remaining attributes, accuracy, and expandability. A new pattern can be added only as a child node of an expandable node. Thus, expandability is the key for regulating the number of patterns.

The root node is always expandable and has negative accuracy. Other than the root node, accuracy of each node is defined from a crowd's feedback; sample evaluation. Our system can extract triples from sentences using a specific pattern and vice versa. So if a crowd feeds back by evaluating samples, our system can backtrack a pattern and update its accuracy. For example, our system extracts the triple (A, *parent*, B) from the sentence "A is the son of B." using a certain pattern P. A crowd may positively evaluate this sample. Then our system adds one more positive answer to feedback history of the pattern P then calculates a new accuracy. Expandability is also updated.

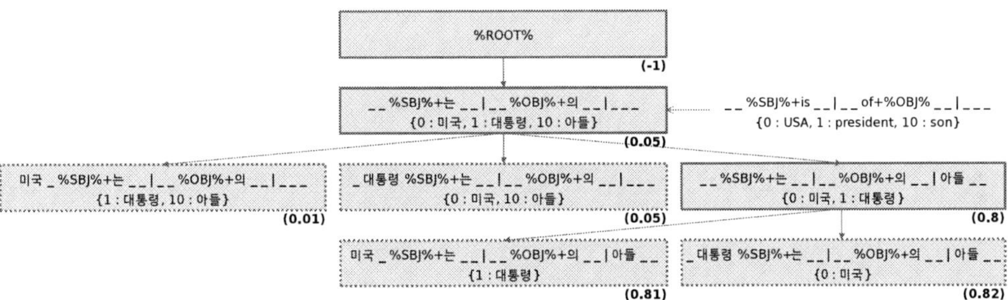

Figure 2: Example of pattern expansion

Now we can track back to the model in Figure 2. The model is grown up from the pattern in Figure 1. First, the pattern is generalized. A generalized pattern contains only two attribute; subject and object with preposition or postposition if any. Attributes other than those two are remaining attributes and separately stored with their positional information. Then RECrowd extracts sample triples with corresponding sentences using the generalized pattern then asks a crowd to evaluate. Whatever accuracy the pattern gets back, the node is expandable since the root node has negative accuracy. Then it can produce a child pattern using its remaining attributes. Next, the first child pattern is added. It has one more attribute than its parent pattern. Since its accuracy is not higher than its parent pattern, it becomes not expandable. The second child pattern is also not expandable for the same reason. We can guess that attributes 'USA' or 'president' do not give much hint to the relation *parent*. However, the third child pattern with additional attribute 'son' has much higher accuracy and remains expandable. Then it can produce next child patterns as you can see. But they are not expandable so the model does not grow anymore.

In pattern matching, an empty attribute means that any lemma can come to its position. This is why a parent pattern is more general than a child pattern. A child pattern unconditionally extracts less triples than its parent pattern. Then the only advantage we can expect when we add a new child pattern to a model is that the child pattern extracts triples with outstanding accuracy. If accuracy does not increase much from parent pattern to child pattern, disadvantage of computational cost cancels out the advantage of having one more pattern. So it is reasonable to stop if a child pattern does not have much higher accuracy. We can define the expandability like the following:

$$Expandability := \left(\frac{\Delta Crowd\ Accuracy}{\Delta \parallel Extracted\ Triples \parallel} \geq threshold \right) \tag{1}$$

3 System Workflow

Workflow of our system is shown in Figure 3. Since our system assigns a different set of patterns for each relation, the workflow starts with relation selection. After a specific relation is chosen, one random pattern is pulled out from patterns to learn or learned patterns. Patterns learned indicate patterns which have been fed back from a crowd so they already have accuracy and expandability. Patterns to learn mean patterns which have not yet received any feedback from a crowd. Once a pattern to learn got feedback from a crowd, then pattern will be added to patterns learned with accuracy and expandability. Using the selected pattern, our system can extract triples from sentences and sample a few triples with corresponding sentences for a crowd to evaluate. A crowd only needs to read a sentence then checks an associated triple is correctly expressed in the sentence. A crowd simply answers whether each triple extraction is correct or not. Since feedback procedure is very easy like this, an inexpert crowd can interact with the system. Extraction with positive answers are uploaded into a knowledge graph. Our system also keeps saving up a crowd's true-false feedback and updating accuracy and expandability. Ancestor and descendant patterns could be recursively updated when certain expandability is changed. Once again a relation extraction model is continuously trained while a knowledge graph is expanded.

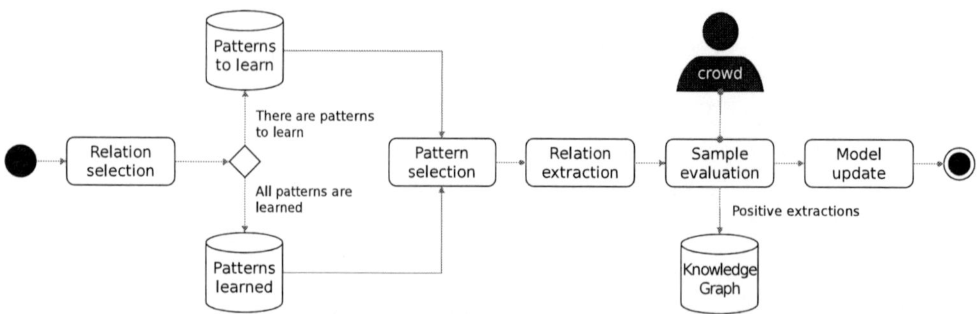

Figure 3: RECrowd workflow

4   Experiment

To see if a relation extraction model in our system is really trained, a small-scale experiment was conducted. Our main focus is to manually trace if a model finds out valid patterns as it grows. We want to guess if a model is capable to achieve this goal when it grows big by inspecting a mini model.

We trained a model for the relation *parent* using 10 randomly chosen sentences from 2400 Korean sentences collected from Korean Wikipedia and Korean DBpedia using distantly supervised approach (Mintz et al, 2009). In training phase, total 112 patterns are generated from the 10 sentences. After 320 sample evaluations were fed back, however, 48 patterns were filtered out as child patterns of not expandable patterns. The trained model contains 64 patterns and 21 patterns were still expandable. In result, all meaningful patterns are still contained in the trained model. Since 320 evaluations are quite small in crowd sourcing, it is a promising result. As Figure 2 shows, a model in our system has a tree structure without much depth. This means that this model quickly reaches to meaningful patterns then efficiently filters out meaningless patterns using stopping condition, the expandability. The rate of filtered out patterns will be larger in a bigger model. In addition, 75 extractions with positive feedback are simply uploaded to a knowledge graph.

5   Conclusion

Existence of good knowledge graphs is essential in question answering system. To upload only correct triples, crowd sourcing may be necessary to validate triples. Our system makes one more use of crowd sourcing; not only to find correct triples to add into a knowledge graph but also to train a relation extraction model. A well trained relation extraction model maximizes efficiency of crowd sourcing; more extractions get positive feedback from a crowd then more triples can be uploaded. Our system is developed using Korean NLP (Natural Language Processing) tool and tested on Korean Wikipedia dump. You can see the demonstration in our demo web page[1].

Acknowledgement

This work was supported by Institute for Information & communications Technology Promotion(IITP) grant funded by the Korea government(MSIP) (No. R0101-16-0054, WiseKB: Big data based self-evolving knowledge base and reasoning platform). This work was supported by the Bio & Medical Technology Development Program of the NRF funded by the Korean government, MSIP(2015M3A9A7029735).

References

Guodong Zhou, Jian Su, Jie Zhang, and Min Zhang. 2005. *Exploring various knowledge in relation extraction*, In ACL 05, pages 427-434. Ann Arbor, MI.

[1]http://143.248.135.210/recrowd

Mike Mintz, Steven Bills, Rion Snow, and Dan Jurafsky. 2009. *Distant supervision for relation extraction without labeled data*, In ACL 2009, pages 1003-1011. Stanford University, Stanford, CA 94305.

Patrick Pantel and Marco Pennacchiotti. 2006. *Espresso: leveraging generic patterns from automatically harvesting semantic relations.*, In COLING/ACL 2006, pages 113-120. Sydney, Australia.

Razvan Bunescu and Raymond Mooney. 2007. *Learning to extract relations from the web using minimal supervision*, In ACL 2007, pages 576-583. Prague, Czech Republic, June.

Pairing Wikipedia Articles Across Languages

Marcus Klang
Lund University
Department of Computer Science
Lund, Sweden
Marcus.Klang@cs.lth.se

Pierre Nugues
Lund University
Department of Computer Science
Lund, Sweden
Pierre.Nugues@cs.lth.se

Abstract

Wikipedia has become a reference knowledge source for scores of NLP applications. One of its invaluable features lies in its multilingual nature, where articles on a same entity or concept can have from one to more than 200 different versions. The interlinking of language versions in Wikipedia has undergone a major renewal with the advent of Wikidata, a unified scheme to identify entities and their properties using unique numbers. However, as the interlinking is still manually carried out by thousands of editors across the globe, errors may creep in the assignment of entities. In this paper, we describe an optimization technique to match automatically language versions of articles, and hence entities, that is only based on bags of words and anchors. We created a dataset of all the articles on persons we extracted from Wikipedia in six languages: English, French, German, Russian, Spanish, and Swedish. We report a correct match of at least 94.3% on each pair.

1 Introduction

Wikipedia has become a major reference knowledge source for applications such as IBM Watson (Ferrucci, 2012) or Google's knowledge graph (Singhal, 2012). Wikipedia is available in more than 280 languages such as Indonesian, Amharic, Nahuatl, or Hindi and its content and coverage are continuously growing thanks to millions of contributors.

One of the major steps to organize the linguistic diversity of Wikipedia has been the creation of Wikidata: A centralized repository of entities and concepts identified by unique numbers. Before Wikidata, an editor creating an article, say on Madagascar in Spanish, had to link it manually to already existing versions of the same entity. Now, Wikidata stores links to all the versions in a centralized repository (Fig. 1) and adding a new language is carried out through this repository and a unique number: Q1019 in the case of Madagascar. In addition to associating unique identifiers to entities, Wikidata uses a set of about 2,500 properties, as of June 1, 2016, to describe them. One of these properties is *instance of*, P31, that enables the editors to define an ontology. Madagascar, for example, is an instance of a sovereign state, an island, an island nation, a country, and a member state of the United Nations (Fig. 1).

Although Wikidata has simplified the linking process, it is still a manual operation that is not error-free and articles may be incorrectly linked across the languages. In this paper, we report and evaluate a technique that, given a human entity, automatically identifies the set of articles describing this entity across six Wikipedia languages: English, French, German, Russian, Spanish, and Swedish. We report a correct match of at least 94.7% for each pair selected among the six versions.

2 Previous Work

Comparable corpora, like the language versions of Wikipedia, have been used extensively as resources to extract word translations or parallel sentences. Rapp et al. (2012) for instance, used Wikipedia articles in nine languages to identify word translations through keywords and a word alignment algorithm. Schamoni et al. (2014) proposed to use links to retrieve Wikipedia articles in English similar to an article

Proceedings of the Open Knowledge Base and Question Answering (OKBQA) Workshop,
pages 72–76, Osaka, Japan, December 11 2016.

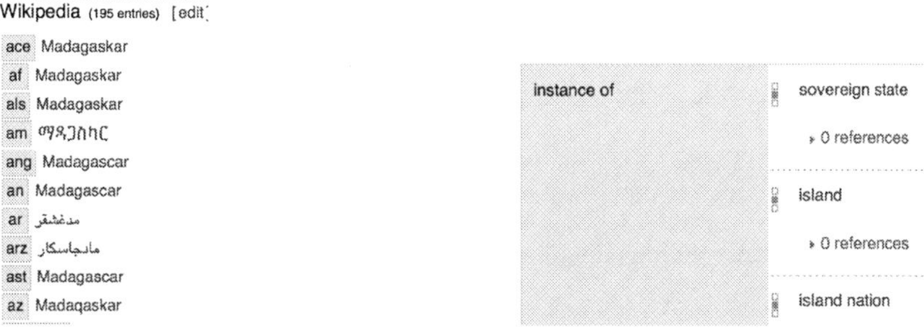

Figure 1: **Left part**: The first language versions of Madagascar in Wikidata. The languages appear in alphabetic order out of 195. **Right part**: Membership of Madagascar to ontology classes using the *instance of* property; three classes are listed out of five

in German. Domínguez García et al. (2012) extracted hyponymy relations from the Wikipedia category system across languages. Chiao and Zweigenbaum (2002) used a set of documents in French and English collected with medical taxonomy terms to produce translational equivalents. Sproat et al. (2006) used English and Chinese stories from the Xinhua News agency to identify named entity transliterations. Finally, Smith et al. (2010) improved translation performance using sets of parallel sentences that they extracted from Wikipedia.

Although these works carry out some kind of matching across languages, we could not find references on a systematic attempt to pair descriptions of an entity in multiple language versions. To the best of our knowledge, we are the first to propose and evaluate a method in this field.

3 Collecting the Corpus

We used six dumps of Wikipedia in English, French, German, Russian, Spanish, and Swedish[1] from which we extracted all the persons. We carried out this extraction using the *instance of* property, where we collected all the articles that had a direct link to the node denoting a human entity (Q5 in Wikidata). Table 1, left part, shows the counts of articles on persons broken down per language.

From this person data set, we extracted all the articles having the six language versions. Again, we used the Wikidata identifier to determine the available language versions of an entity. We obtained a total of 1,938,861 unique persons having at least one version in one of the six languages and where 39,636 had versions in the six languages (Table 1, right part).

Language	Count	Language	Count	Versions	Count	Versions	Count
en	1,257,604	ru	297,202	6	39,636	3	115,692
de	579,656	es	262,538	5	42,986	2	284,658
fr	446,308	sv	178,894	4	65,725	1	1,390,164

Table 1: **Left part**: Counts of articles on persons per language version. **Right part**: Number of versions for the articles on persons

4 Method

To implement the comparison method, we restricted the articles to their first paragraphs that we represented as bags of words and entity identifiers (Wikidata Q-number). For a given pair of languages, we then determined the best pair of paragraphs using the cosine similarity.

The articles on persons in Wikipedia show a similar structure, where the first paragraph starts with the name of the person and reports a few basic facts such as the dates and places of birth and death using

---

[1]Retrieved in May and September 2015.

numbers and proper nouns. In languages using the Gregorian calendar, the numbers are often the same across the versions and many proper nouns also have identical forms and spellings.

For instance, the first paragraph on Shakespeare in the French Wikipedia,

> **William Shakespeare**, né probablement le **26** avril **1564** à Stratford-upon-**Avon** et mort le 3 mai (**23** avril) **1616** dans la même ville, [...] à représenter les aspects de la nature humaine.

shares seven words with the corresponding paragraph in English:

> **William Shakespeare** (/ˈʃeɪkspɪər/; **26** April **1564** (baptised) – **23** April **1616**) was an English poet, playwright, and actor, [...] and the "Bard of **Avon**" [...] than those of any other playwright.

while it does not share a single word with Napoléon's one:

> Napoléon Bonaparte (/nəˈpoʊliən, -ˈpoʊljən/; French: [napoleɔ̃ bɔnapaʁt], born Napoleone di Buonaparte; 15 August 1769 – 5 May 1821) was a French military and political leader [...] Napoleon implemented foundational liberal reforms in France and throughout Europe. [...]

We represented each article as a bag of words of its first paragraph with the vector space model (Salton et al., 1974). In addition to the words, we used resolved anchors from the first paragraph with their Q-numbers as terms. We extracted all the unique tokens and Q-numbers from all the documents from which we excluded 250 stop words that we defined as the words that occur in the highest number of documents across the four versions. We used this variant of $TF \cdot IDF$: $weight(\text{term}) = tf(\text{term}, d) \cdot \log \frac{N}{df(\text{term}, D)}$, where tf is the term frequency in the current document d (a paragraph); df is the document frequency, that is the number of paragraphs D that contain this term; N is the total number of documents; in our case, the total number of paragraphs.

Given a pair of languages, the two sets of articles in their respective languages and their association form a weighted bipartite graph, where the comparison (matching) step can be formulated as a linear assignment problem (Jacobi, 1865; Kuhn, 1955; Jonker and Volgenant, 1987). The worst case of computing the weight matrix involves $O(N^2)$ operations, which for our dataset corresponds to 1.57 billion operations, while the assignment problem has a $O(N^3)$ worst case complexity. This figure is still in the realm of feasibility, but could quickly get worse with more categories. Fortunately, our comparisons involve pairs that typically share few terms, and most often none at all. In this case, their cosine similarity is 0. In our data set, 95% of the matrix elements are zero, which makes the computation of an optimal solution tractable using a sparse linear assignment algorithm.

5 Exploratory Analysis

Taking advantage of the sparsity, we conducted an exploratory analysis and a preliminary evaluation. We compared paragraphs that shared at least one term and we implemented a simplified assignment algorithm that reduced drastically the number of operations. Given a pair of languages, the source and the target, we compared each document from the source with all the target documents that shared at least one term with it and we assigned the target document that had the maximal similarity. This simplified assignment corresponds to the initial cover in Kuhn (1955).

We applied the comparison algorithm to the set of articles. For all the language pairs, the number of misclassified articles is less than 17.0%, a surprisingly low figure for such a simple method. Table 2 shows the results, where the most confused language pair is French–English and the less one, Swedish–German.

We also examined the influence of the cosine similarity on the method using the precision and recall scores. We applied a cutoff to this similarity to validate a pair that we varied between 0 and 1. Figure 2 shows the recall and precision on the Swedish–French pair with respect to this cutoff. All the other pairs show a similar pattern. A cutoff of 0 always selects the highest cosine similarity whatever its value, while a 1 will request the paragraphs to have exactly the same words. We can see that a very high recall is reached without cutoff, while the precision is moderately improved by it. A perfect precision is reached when the cosine similarity is greater than 0.76, while a high cutoff discards all the pairs.

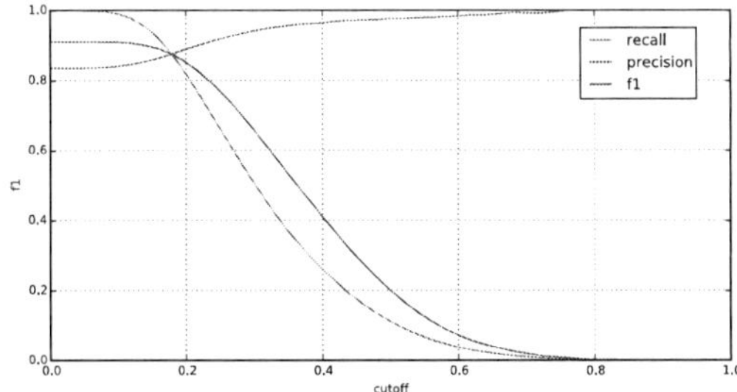

Figure 2: Recall and precision with respect to the cutoff for the Swedish–English pair

	de	en	es	fr	ru	sv
de	–	15.5	8.6	6.6	9.7	6.3
en	11.8	–	13.6	14.8	14.9	13.9
es	6.0	14.5	–	8.4	12.8	8.4
fr	5.3	17.0	9.9	–	12.7	8.7
ru	7.1	14.8	11.4	10.3	–	10.7
sv	5.0	16.4	10.0	8.7	13.4	–

Table 2: Percentages of misclassified pairs using the naïve method. First column: source language; first row: target language

	de	en	es	fr	ru	sv	avg
de	–	2.0	1.9	1.7	3.1	1.0	1.9
en	2.0	–	3.2	3.2	5.0	2.6	3.2
es	2.0	3.1	–	2.6	4.8	2.4	3.0
fr	1.7	3.2	2.6	–	4.7	2.4	2.9
ru	3.1	5.0	4.8	4.6	–	5.7	4.7
sv	0.9	2.6	2.4	2.4	4.9	–	2.7

Table 3: Percentages of misclassified pairs using the linear assignment algorithm.

6 Linear Assignment

Finally, we applied the sparse linear assignment algorithm by Jonker and Volgenant (1987) to all the pairs in our data set using a modified version of the Fiji library from Schindelin et al. (2012). For each pair, we excluded the documents that shared no word and we applied the algorithm to the resulting matrix. In spite of the matrix sizes (nearly $40,000 \times 40,000$) and the algorithm complexity, the run time to compute an assignment matrix takes less than two hours on Intel Xeon desktop computer. Table 3 shows the results, where the most confused language pair is Russian–Swedish and the less one, Swedish–German.

7 Discussion and Conclusion

The matching method we proposed shows it could reach a high accuracy with a standard bag-of-word technique, including words and entity identifiers, even with the simplified assignment method. This surprisingly high accuracy is due to the similar structure adopted by most articles on persons in their first paragraph. The proper nouns and the dates this paragraph contains proved to be sufficiently discriminative to have error rates less than 5.7% across the languages.

We applied this method to languages having the highest number of views per hour on Wikipedia[2], English and Spanish, as well as French and Swedish, that show no or little proper noun inflection, and hence where the proper nouns are identical across the versions. Nonetheless, the errors we obtained with Russian, if larger, are still comparable to those we got with the other languages: The pair (en, fr) shows an error of 3.2%, while (en, ru) is of 5.0%, for instance. Such results can be explained by the Q-numbers appearing in the bag-of-word vectors that are shared by the languages of a pair, whatever the script or morphology. They suggest this method is applicable to nonLatin scripts or to languages with a richer inflection. We believe this technique paves the way for an automatic matching of comparable textual resources across languages as well as interactive tools to support the creation and linking of new articles.

Acknowledgments

This research was supported by Vetenskapsrådet, the Swedish research council, under the *Det digitaliserade samhället* program.

---

[2] http://stats.wikimedia.org/

References

Yun-Chuang Chiao and Pierre Zweigenbaum. 2002. Looking for candidate translational equivalents in specialized, comparable corpora. In *Proceedings of the 19th International Conference on Computational Linguistics - Volume 2*, COLING '02, pages 1–5.

Renato Domínguez García, Sebastian Schmidt, Christoph Rensing, and Ralf Steinmetz, 2012. *Computational Linguistics and Intelligent Text Processing: 13th International Conference, CICLing 2012, New Delhi, India, March 11-17, 2012, Proceedings, Part I*, chapter Automatic Taxonomy Extraction in Different Languages Using Wikipedia and Minimal Language-Specific Information, pages 42–53. Springer Berlin Heidelberg, Berlin, Heidelberg.

David Angelo Ferrucci. 2012. Introduction to "This is Watson". *IBM Journal of Research and Development*, 56(3.4):1:1 –1:15, May-June.

Carl Jacobi. 1865. De investigando ordine systematis aequationum differentialum vulgarium cujuscunque. *Journal für die reine und angewandte Mathematik*, 64:297–320.

Roy Jonker and Anton Volgenant. 1987. A shortest augmenting path algorithm for dense and sparse linear assignment problems. *Computing*, 38(4):325–340.

Harold W. Kuhn. 1955. The Hungarian method for the assignment problem. *Naval Research Logistics Quarterly*, 2:83–97.

Reinhard Rapp, Serge Sharoff, and Bogdan Babych. 2012. Identifying word translations from comparable documents without a seed lexicon. In *Proceedings of the Eighth International Conference on Language Resources and Evaluation (LREC-2012)*, pages 460–466, Istanbul, Turkey, May.

Gerard Salton, A. Wong, and C. S. Yang. 1974. A vector space model for automatic indexing. Technical Report TR74-218, Department of Computer Science, Cornell University, Ithaca, New York.

Shigehiko Schamoni, Felix Hieber, Artem Sokolov, and Stefan Riezler. 2014. Learning translational and knowledge-based similarities from relevance rankings for cross-language retrieval. In *Proceedings of the 52nd Annual Meeting of the Association for Computational Linguistics (Volume 2: Short Papers)*, pages 488–494, Baltimore, Maryland, June. Association for Computational Linguistics.

Johannes Schindelin, Ignacio Arganda-Carreras, Erwin Frise, Verena Kaynig, Mark Longair, Tobias Pietzsch, Stephan Preibisch, Curtis Rueden, Stephan Saalfeld, Benjamin Schmid, Jean-Yves Tinevez, Daniel James White, Volker Hartenstein, Kevin Eliceiri, Pavel Tomancak, and Albert Cardona. 2012. Fiji: an open-source platform for biological-image analysis. *Nature Methods*, 9(7):676–682, 07.

Amit Singhal. 2012. Introducing the knowledge graph: things, not strings. Official Google Blog. `http://googleblog.blogspot.com/2012/05/introducing-knowledge-graph-things-not.html`, May.

Jason R. Smith, Chris Quirk, and Kristina Toutanova. 2010. Extracting parallel sentences from comparable corpora using document level alignment. In *Human Language Technologies: The 2010 Annual Conference of the North American Chapter of the Association for Computational Linguistics*, HLT '10, pages 403–411.

Richard Sproat, Tao Tao, and ChengXiang Zhai. 2006. Named entity transliteration with comparable corpora. In *Proceedings of the 21st International Conference on Computational Linguistics and 44th Annual Meeting of the Association for Computational Linguistics*, pages 73–80, Sydney, Australia, July.

SRDF: Extracting Lexical Knowledge Graph for Preserving Sentence Meaning

Sangha Nam, GyuHyeon Choi, Younggyun Hahm, and **Key-Sun Choi**
Machine Reading Lab, School of Computing,
Korea Advanced Institute of Science and Technology (KAIST),
Daejeon, Republic of Korea
{nam.sangha, wiany11, hahmyg, kschoi}@kaist.ac.kr

Abstract

In this paper, we present an open information extraction system so-called SRDF that generates lexical knowledge graphs from unstructured texts. In semantic web, knowledge is expressed in the RDF triple form but the natural language text consist of multiple relations between arguments. For this reason, we combine open information extraction with the reification for the full text extraction to preserve the meaning of sentences in our knowledge graph. And also our knowledge graph is designed to adapt for many existing semantic web applications. At the end of this paper, we introduce the result of an experiment and a Korean template generation module developed using SRDF.

1 Introduction

The web contains enormous information in the form of unstructured text. In recent years, Open Information Extraction (IE) based on self-supervised learning has become more strongly suggested to overcome limitations of traditional IE system, and it is now possible to process massive text corpora. However, early Open IE systems fall short of representing multiple relations between arguments within a sentence since they are designed to focus on binary extractions. This causes incomplete and insufficient extraction. To overcome this limitations, Kraken(Akbik and Löser, 2012), OLLIE(Mausam et al., 2012) and ClausIE(Del Corro and Gemulla, 2013) are designed to extract a set of arguments using dependency parsing and then represent the extracted knowledge as ternary or N-ary form.

Consider, for example, the sentence *"Marsel was established by the British government with the help of American policymakers in 1971 as the nation's first research oriented science institution."*. Current Open IE systems focus on extracting triples; (*Marsel, was established by, the British government*) and (*Marsel, was established in, 1971*). Even if these systems extract multiple triples, there is still missing information. The arguments *'help of American policymakers'* and *'the nation's first research oriented science institution'* are also important and necessary information for a question answering system when a question becomes more complicated. Furthermore, it is important to represent extracted knowledge for applying to existing semantic web applications.

In this paper, we propose an Open Information Extraction system so-called SRDF that generates lexical knowledge graph from unstructured texts. SRDF differs from other Open IE systems in terms of full sentence extraction and knowledge representation in reified triple form. In semantic web, knowledge is commonly expressed in RDF triple form that consists of subject, predicate and object. However, there are a lot of cases that multiple relations between arguments are associated within a sentence. The purpose of SRDF is to make a bridge between text and triple by the lexical knowledge graph. Not only does SRDF knowledge graph (KG) reflect the dependency structure of a sentence but can also be used in a variety of semantic web applications such as question answering.

2 What is SRDF?

77

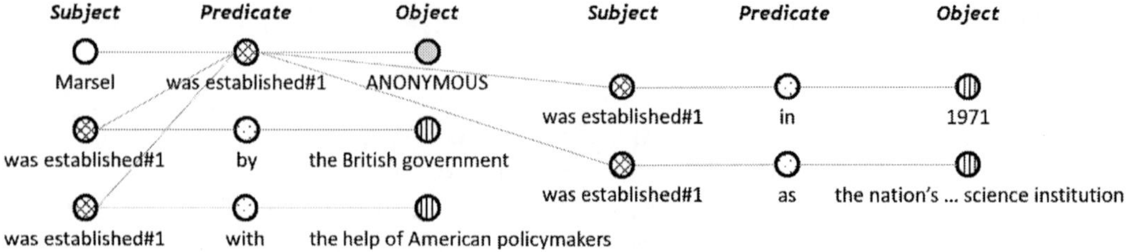

Figure 1: Example of SRDF knowledge graph

Extracting ontological triples directly from the text needs many steps such as entity linking, disambiguation and predicate linking, and also needs many resources like *Wordnet*. Nevertheless, usual performance is still unsatisfiable because the whole process is complicated and errors of each step propagating to the next step. That is why Open IE has been researched.

The purpose of SRDF generates a lexical knowledge graph as a bridge between text and triple. SRDF means sentence-based lexical knowledge graph structure. SRDF structure serves three purposes. First, it translates an input sentence to reified triple form with simple and concise rules and reflects the dependency structure of the sentence. Second, it supports handling both entity-centric and event-centric facts. Third, it is designed to be used in various semantic web applications.

As mentioned earlier, multiple arguments and relations are presented within a sentence, so we design our structure using *Singleton Property*(Nguyen et al., 2014) - the new method of reification. The main idea of *Singleton Property* is that every relationship is universally unique, so the predicate between two particular entities can be a key for any triple.

Figure 1 is an example of SRDF a knowledge graph from the sentence described in the introduction. As shown in Figure 1, SRDF follows a triple form. The reason for taking triple form is a versatility. Triple is the simplest semantic web representation form, moreover many semantic web applications such as knowledge base and question answering systems take the triple form. Therefore we extract the knowledge in triple form for integration with existing applications easily. As a knowledge graph, SRDF also consists of triples but of different properties followed by:

- **Subject** can only be the subject of the sentence or reified predicate.
- **Predicate** can only be the verb group of the sentence or pre/postposition of its objects.
- **Object** can only be the noun group or ANONYMOUS.

3   Overview and Workflow Description

SRDF system simply receives input as a text and outputs an extracted set of reified triples. Our system operates through three steps of procedure in total that are Preprocessor, Basic Skeleton Tree (BST) generator, and SRDF generator. Detailed explanations are following as shown in Figure 2.

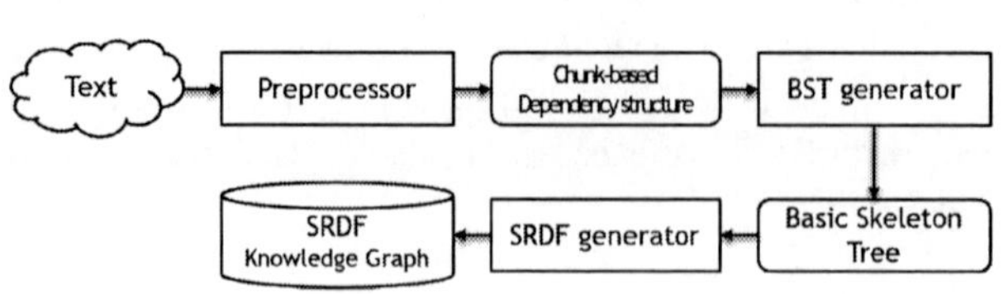

Figure 2: System architecture of SRDF

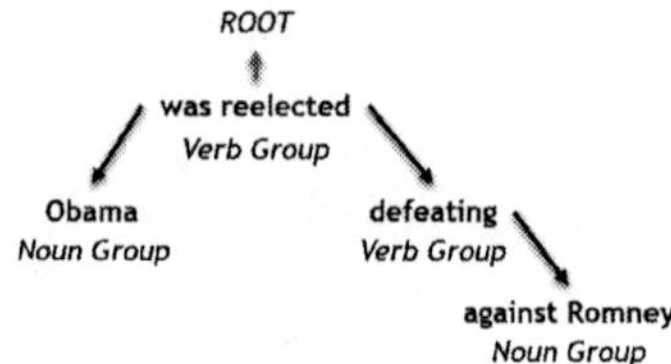

Figure 3: Example of chunk-based dependency structure

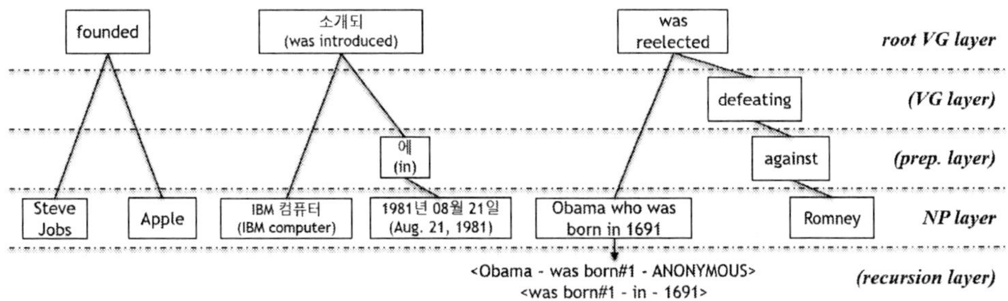

Figure 4: Three examples of Basic Skeleton Tree in SRDF

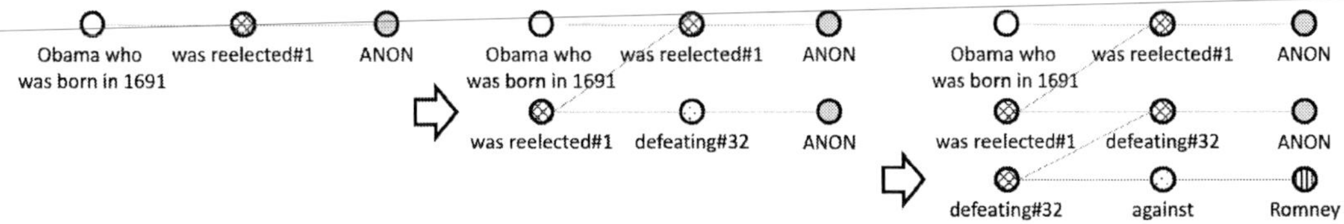

Figure 5: Example of SRDF reified triple generation

3.1 Preprocessor

Preprocessor consists of three sub-modules which are Sentence segmentor, Chunker, and Dependency parser. Sentence segmentor divides a sentence into its component sentences and attaches the subject to divided sentences. Chunker returns only noun phrases and verb groups. Noun phrases can contain adnominal phrase and verb groups could contain adverb phrase. Then, dependency parser outputs a chunk-based dependency structure like figure 3.

3.2 Basic Skeleton Tree Generator

BST generator takes an input as a chunk-based dependency structure and outputs a BST. Chunk-based dependency structure strongly depends on charasteristics of languages. For example, dependency structure of English, Korean and Chinese are different from one another. Therefore we make an intermediate structure between chunk-based dependency structure and SRDF. BST would be almost the same structure for any language could be adjusted to SRDF generation rules as well.

Figure 4 is examples of the Basic Skeleton Tree. BST has five layers; root-VG, VG, NP, preposition and recursion layer. Root-VG layer is the top layer and has only one node that is root verb group on dependency structure. NP layer contains all noun phrases including subject of the sentence. VG layer is placed between the root-VG and the NP layer. There could be more than one VG layers relying on depth of corresponding verb groups in chunk-based dependency structure. Preposition layer contains only preposition of its noun phrase and be placed over the NP layer. Recursion layer decomposes noun phrase with more detail when it contains adnominal phrase.

3.3 SRDF Generator

SRDF generator takes an input as a BST and outputs a lexical knowledge graph as reified triple form using our simple and concise algorithm as shown in Algorithm 1. It takes a graph *G*, a subject of sentence *sbj*, a root verb group *pred*, and child nodes of root verb group *objQueue* as input and returns *G*. For each *obj* in *objQueue*, check whether it is in NP layer or not. If the *obj* is in NP layer, make a triple and insert it to graph *G* (Line 4). If not, make an *ANON* triple and insert it to *G* and then change *sbj* and *pred* respectively for reification (Line 6 to 8). And then, call *generateSRDF* function recursively (Line 9). Figure 5 is an example of our algorithm about the third BST in Figure 4.

Algorithm 1 SRDF reified triple generation algorithm

```
 1: procedure GENERATESRDF(G, SBJ, PRED, OBJQUEUE)
 2:     for obj in objQueue do
 3:         if obj is in NP layer then
 4:             G ← G ∪ {<sbj,pred,obj>}   ▷ Overwrite ANON object with the same sbj and pred
 5:         else
 6:             G ← G ∪ {<sbj,pred,ANON>}
 7:             sbj ← pred
 8:             pred ← obj
 9:             generateSRDF(G, sbj, pred, obj.children)
10:     return G
```

Table 1: Results of experiments.

Precision	Recall	Completeness
0.74	0.75	0.93
301/407	251/336	128/137

4 Experiments and Application

4.1 Experiments

The performance of SRDF system has been evaluated with randomly sampled sentences from featured article in *Korean Wikipedia*. The evaluation results have been assessed by two human evaluators based on the precision, recall and the number of extractions. As shown in Table 1, our system extracted 407 triples from 137 sentences. The precision is 74% and the recall is 75%. The completeness means if all the information is extracted as triples from an input sentence or not. Overall completeness is 93%. We found that the 7% of incomplete extractions is caused by the Korean Analyzer, especially a problem of correctly finding the subject of a given sentence. In our experimental results, the precision and recall are similar to recent open information extraction systems' but our system can extract all information from the input sentence. Through the results, we assume that SRDF could be useful in QA task for a relatively long question.

4.2 SenTGM in OKBQA platform

Open Knowledge Base and Question Answering (OKBQA) is a community and a hackathon to make advanced technology for developing a question answering system. The virtue of OKBQA is open collaboration that harmonize resources developed by different groups scattered over the world. We made SenTGM for the first step of OKBQA called Template Generation using our SRDF system. SenTGM takes a Korean natural language question and produces a pseudo query defined in Templator (Unger et al., 2012) and it is now working for the Korean natural language question in OKBQA framework properly. The architecture and example of SenTGM is shown in Figure 6.

5 Conclusion

In this paper, we proposed a new open information extraction system called SRDF. Our approach is a novel method of combining Open IE with the singleton property technique for the full text extraction. Furthermore SRDF represents extracted knowledge as reified triple form for usability in many existing semantic web applications. And also we demonstrated that our approach can be used in the OKBQA framework for question answering. In the future, we will research a question answering approach over SRDF knowledge graph using the synonym such as Wordnet and word embedding to resolve the ambiguity.

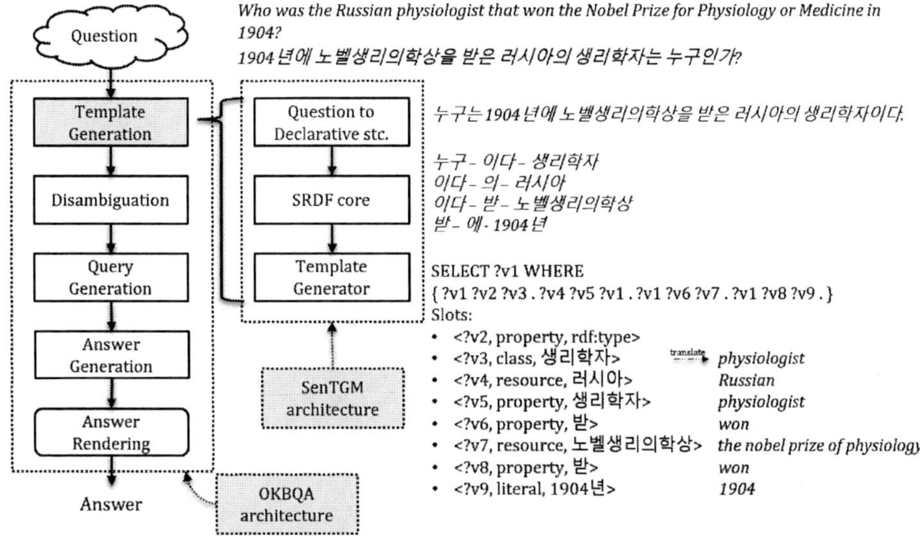

Figure 6: Architecture and Example of SenTGM

Acknowledgement

This work was supported by Institute for Information & communications Technology Promotion(IITP) grant funded by the Korea government(MSIP) (No. R0101-16-0054, WiseKB: Big data based self-evolving knowledge base and reasoning platform). This work was supported by the Bio & Medical Technology Development Program of the NRF funded by the Korean government, MSIP(2015M3A9A7029735)

References

Alan Akbik and Alexander Löser. 2012. Kraken: N-ary facts in open information extraction. In *Proceedings of the Joint Workshop on Automatic Knowledge Base Construction and Web-scale Knowledge Extraction*, AKBC-WEKEX '12, pages 52–56, Stroudsburg, PA, USA. Association for Computational Linguistics.

Luciano Del Corro and Rainer Gemulla. 2013. Clausie: Clause-based open information extraction. In *Proceedings of the 22Nd International Conference on World Wide Web*, WWW '13, pages 355–366, New York, NY, USA. ACM.

Mausam, Michael Schmitz, Robert Bart, Stephen Soderland, and Oren Etzioni. 2012. Open language learning for information extraction. In *Proceedings of the 2012 Joint Conference on Empirical Methods in Natural Language Processing and Computational Natural Language Learning*, EMNLP-CoNLL '12, pages 523–534, Stroudsburg, PA, USA. Association for Computational Linguistics.

Vinh Nguyen, Olivier Bodenreider, and Amit Sheth. 2014. Don't like rdf reification?: making statements about statements using singleton property. In *Proceedings of the 23rd international conference on World wide web*, pages 759–770. ACM.

Christina Unger, Lorenz Bühmann, Jens Lehmann, Axel-Cyrille Ngonga Ngomo, Daniel Gerber, and Philipp Cimiano. 2012. Template-based question answering over rdf data. In *Proceedings of the 21st international conference on World Wide Web*, pages 639–648. ACM.

QAF: Frame Semantics-based Question Interpretation

Younggyun Hahm, Sangha Nam, Key-Sun Choi
Machine Reading Lab
KAIST
Republic of Korea
{hahmyg, nam.sangha, kschoi}@kaist.ac.kr

Abstract

Natural language questions are interpreted to a sequence of patterns to be matched with instances of patterns in a knowledge base (KB) for answering. A natural language (NL) question answering (QA) system utilizes meaningful patterns matching the syntactic/lexical features between the NL questions and KB. In the most of KBs, there are only binary relations in triple form to represent relation between two entities or entity and a value using the domain specific ontology. However, the binary relation representation is not enough to cover complex information in questions, and the ontology vocabulary sometimes does not cover the lexical meaning in questions. Complex meaning needs a knowledge representation to link the binary relation-type triples in KB. In this paper, we propose a frame semantics-based semantic parsing approach as KB-independent question pre-processing. We will propose requirements of question interpretation in the KBQA perspective, and a query form representation based on our proposed format *QAF (Question Answering with the Frame Semantics)*, which is supposed to cover the requirements. In QAF, frame semantics roles as a model to represent complex information in questions and to disambiguate the lexical meaning in questions to match with the ontology vocabulary. Our system takes a question as an input and outputs QAF-query by the process which assigns semantic information in the question to its corresponding frame semantic structure using the semantic parsing rules.

1 Introduction

Nowadays, there are many ongoing researches to build a knowledge base question answering (KBQA) system with the growing interest of KBs such as Freebase (Bollacker *et al.*, 2008), DBpedia (Auer et al., 2007) and YAGO2 (Hoffart *et al.*, 2011). Most of KBs consist of structured data in triple form <s, p, o>, and SPARQL query is used to access triple data. However, for common users, it is required to learn query language and the schemas underlying KBs. Thus, providing intuitive interfaces for KBQA is an important task to help users access the massive amount of information in KB. Question interpretation is an essential task to generate the suitable query to answer natural language questions by translating it. And there are many research efforts such as QALD[1] and OKBQA[2] to address this problem.

Traditionally, to translate natural language question into machine readable query, there are two major approaches, the information extraction approach and the semantic parsing approach (Yao *et al.*, 2014a). The information extraction (IE) approach learns meaningful patterns and rules by matching the syntactic structure of question with the schemas in KB, and the lexical features with the ontology vocabulary in KB (Yao *et al.*, 2014b). This process is based on the traditional IE approach such as a distant supervision

---

[1] http://qald.sebastianwalter.org/
[2] http://www.okbqa.org/

Proceedings of the Open Knowledge Base and Question Answering (OKBQA) Workshop,
pages 82–90, Osaka, Japan, December 11 2016.

(Mintz *et al.*, 2009), and it generates KB specified query. For example, to answer the example question "Who was the first person reached the South Pole?" over the target KB, the IE approach extracts triples from the question based on the schema underlying target KB. Let's consider DBpedia as the target KB to answer the example question. In DBpedia, there is knowledge to answer the question that exists in the triple form `<dbr:Roald_Amundsen, dbo:knownFor, dbr:South_Pole>`. First, a IE-based system searches sentences which includes the entities, `dbr:Roald_Amundsen` and `dbr:South_Pole`. If a sentence "…Roald Amundsen was the first Norwegian explorer to reach the South Pole…" is discovered, then the system learns patterns syntactic/lexical features by matching the sentence and the triple. For instance, if there are three conditions in a sentence; 1) a word "reach" in a sentence, 2) a subject is PERSON, and 3) an object is LOCATION, a triple is generated by using a pattern rule; `<subject, dbo:knownFor, object>`.

This SPARQL would be supposed suitable to answer the example question over DBpedia;

```
SELECT ?x WHERE {
       ?x      rdf:type     dbo:Person        .
       ?x      dbo:knownFor dbr:South_Pole    . }
```

In the above SPARQL query, `rdf:type` and `dbo:knownFor` are properties in ontology, and `dbo:Person` is a class in ontology. Expected query result is an entity `dbr:Roald_Amundsen`, which is matched with variable `?x` in the two triple patterns, `<?x, rdf:type, dbo:Person>` and `<?x dbo:knownFor dbr:South_Pole>`.

In the example question and its SPARQL, the interrogative word "who" is considered as a variable `?x` in query, and its type is expected to be `dbo:Person` in combination with the word "person" in question. By using the triple pattern `<?x, rdf:type, dbo:Person>`, SPARQL can represent the query intention: '*the expected answer would be a person*'. The IE-based approach extracts the triple pattern `<?x dbo:knownFor dbr:South_Pole>` from the example question by matching the syntactic/lexical features in the example question to DBpedia.

In this case, the property `dbo:knownFor` is used to represent the relationship between two entities; `?x` and `dbr:South_Pole`. The relation is extracted by using the syntactic features such as the grammatical role and named entity, and by using the lexical features such as the meaning of the verb, in this case, "reached". The word "reached" is used to disambiguate the relation and match it with the property `dbo:knownFor`. This IE-based question interpretation is a model with focusing target KB. It would be easy to learn patterns for the specified domain KBs.

However, the IE-based approach involves a limitation of the number of learnable rules because of not only the lack of the ontology vocabulary (Berant *et al.*, 2014) but also the way of expression of knowledge. First, the lack of the ontology vocabulary involves the lack of coverage for the scope of question interpretation. Especially, in our example, DBpedia is constructed under the its own schema, DBpedia Ontology. It is based on the Wikipedia and Infobox (Auer *et al.*, 2007), thus it is suitable to represent factual knowledge such as *NAME, JOB, POPULATION, HEIGHT*, and *NATIONALITY*, because of the characteristic of the Wikipedia as an encyclopedia. However, for the example question, there are irregular mappings between the word "reached" and the ontology vocabulary because of the absence of the proper property to represent the meaning of "reach". By this reason, the word "reach" sometimes would be mapped with the several properties such as `dbo:location`, `dbo:residence`, `dbo:knownFor`, and even `dbo:wikiPageExternalLink`. It is a reason why there is the limitation to interpret the question enough in the KB-dependent approach (Hahm *et al.*, 2014). Second, there is the gap between natural language and structured data in the perspective of the expressiveness. In other words, natural language represents complex information underlying its various syntactic/semantic structure, however, structured data represents information using its schema. In the RDF syntax, there are many ways to represent complex information, such as the attributes of the relation. In our SPARQL example, the variable `?x` has a relation `dbo:knownFor` with the entity `dbr:South_Pole`. To represent more information shown in the example question, the relation `dbo:knownFor` would have an attribute, for example, 'something `?x` is known for the South Pole **as the first person** to reach'.

However, in most of KBs, there are only binary relations in triple form to represent relation between two entities. Therefore, for instance, even we have these two triples; `<dbr:Roald_Amundsen,`

`dbo:knownFor, dbr:South_Pole>` and `<dbr:Roald_Amundsen, isa, first_man>`, we don't know information for 'dbr:Roald_Amindsen is known for South_Pole as the first person' because of the absence of the relation between the property `dbo:knownFor` and the concept of "first man". Thus the specific KB-dependent approach has the limitation of the scope of representable knowledge, in our example, the attribute of the relation.

By contrast, the semantic parsing (SP) is considered the KB-independent approach to analyse user's intention and semantics of information in questions (Xu *et al.*, 2014). The SP approach is not dependent on the specific KB, so that it is efficient on the open domain question answering (Yao *et al.*, 2014a). In this paper, we propose SP approach based on the frame semantics in FrameNet (Baker *et al.*, 1998) to interpret questions. FrameNet uses a PropBank-style predicate-argument structure to represent relations between each argument. Each relation evoked by *target* words, and each relation is disambiguated by assigning the target words to the frames. For instance, in our example question, the word "reached" roles as a *target* and evokes the frame `Arriving` (`frame:Arriving`), and the word "first" also evokes the frame `First_experience` (`frame:First_experience`). The frame is a lexicon to represent not only encyclopedia-like information similar to DBpedia Ontology, but also linguistic level semantics for various information such as *CAUSE & EFFECT, EMOTION, OPINION, MOTION, PROBLEM & SO-LUTION* and so on. These frames would be used for bottom-up grounding of knowledge to interpret questions in the perspective of KBQA, and is used for the ontology vocabulary model for KB directly (Vossen *et al.*, 2014; Rouces *et al.*, 2015). In this paper, as an approach to interpret questions, our goal is to generate the model for machine readable query based on the frames, and our scope is to analyse the single sentence factoid Korean questions as the first step of KBQA system.

To achieve our goal, in Section 2 we will propose the requirements of question interpretation and define the logical form query, QAF, which is supposed to cover the requirements. We designed the frame-based semantic parsing rules for Koran questions in Section 3, and the evaluation result and discussion are described in Section 4.

2   Question Interpretation based on the Frame Semantics

In this section, we define QAF based on the frames for query which are interpreted from NL questions. QAF is designed to cover the requirements of question interpretation in KBQA system.

2.1   Requirements of Question Interpretation

To translate questions into a machine readable queries, there are some requirements which should be analysed. For example, the question:

What was the naval warfare commanded by Admiral Yi Sun-sin at Myeongyang Strait in 1597?

The proper SPARQL query which is translated from the question to get answer from DBpedia would be:

```
SELECT ?x WHERE {
        ?x      rdf:type        dbo:MilitaryConflict      .
        ?x      dbo:commander   "Admiral Yi Sun-sin"      .
        ?x      dbo:place       "Myongyang Strait"        .
        ?x      dbo:date        "1597-00-00"             . }
```

Traditionally, KBQA considers the following three elements as the major things in the question interpretation task (Yao *et al.*, 2014b).

(1) Expected answer type (in our example, dbo:MilitaryConflict)
(2) Question words (What)
(3) Clues of the question (who is commander, where occurred at, when occurred in)

In most of KBs, each entity is defined by using an ontology class (e.g. PERSON, LOCATION, EVENT, and so on), and it is useful to reduce the search space and to select the more disambiguated entities in the process of selecting answer candidates. Thus, in the question interpretation task, the process which identifies and disambiguates the expected answer type in requirement (1) is a major subtask. Also identification of question words in requirement (2) is used to figure out user's intention. The SPARQL query differs for each question words such as "how many", "what is the highest" and "who", in the different way to get answers (Unger *et al.*, 2012). The clues of questions in requirement (3) is written in a triple pattern, `<?answer, p, o>` in the SPARQL query, to find the variable `?answer` in KB. In this paper, we define QAF as a model which covers these requirements, and we developed a question interpretation system which assigns the requirements in questions to the frame structure using the semantic parsing rules that we experimented for the Korean question.

2.2 QAF: Question Answering with the Frame Semantics

Before developing our question interpretation system, we examine the dataset so-called NLQ400 which is used for (Nam *et al.*, 2015). NLQ400 consists of the 384 Korean questions which covers various domains, such as history, science, art, and so on. We choose 95 factoid questions which could be answered by using one single sentence in Wikipedia, and then choose 72 questions excepting multiple choice questions and O/X questions. And then we manually annotate frames for the 72 questions to figure out how to use frames for question answering. For our example question, the frame annotation result is:

Figure 1 An Example of Frame Annotation for Korean Question

In Figure 1, for our example question "What was the naval warfare commanded by Admiral Yi Sun-sin at Myeongyang Strait in 1597?", the word "the naval warfare" is a *target* word which evokes the `frame:Event`, and the semantic role of its arguments are defined by using each frame element (FE) in the `frame:Event`, such as `fe:time`, `fe:place`. In this result, the question word "What" is annotated as a FE (i.e. fe:event). And, in the annotation 2, the word "command" evokes the `frame:Leadership`, and each FE is; leader:"Admiral Yi Sun-sin", time:"1597", place:"Myeongyang Strait", and activity: "the naval warfare". In this case the question word "What" does not annotated as a FE in the annotation 2.

By these annotations, we figure out (1) the expected answer type and (2) the question word are annotated in the annotation 1, and (3) the clues of the question is in the annotation 2. All of 72 questions is annotated in the case of annotation 1. And the word for identification of the expected answer type "the naval warfare" is a node which connects each annotation. Thus, in QAF, the case of annotation 1 would be a basic graph to represent questions in the structured format, and the other annotations are connected with the annotation 1 by using the word for the expected answer type.

We define some terms: the word for the connecting node "the naval warfare" as Q-frame, and the question word "What" as Q-FE, and the clues of questions as Sub-Frame, which is the `frame:Leadership` and its FEs in our example.

The resulting graph for Figure 1 is a representation for QAF (Question Answering with Frame Semantics) to satisfy the requirements. Section 3 is about developing QAF for Korean QA.

3 Frame-semantic Parsing of Question Sentence

3.1 Scope of development

To develop the Korean question interpretation system, we list up the several goals:

Use less amount of training data

English FrameNet[3] is a well-constructed lexicon in its long history, and there are many well-performing frame semantic parsers (Das *et al.*, 2010) using 19,582 target words in 154,607 sample sentences and 3,256 training data sentences in FrameNet. For Korean, there is Korean FrameNet corpus which is constructed by (Park *et al.*, 2014), which had 6,802 target words in 5,507 sentences. However, it is the insufficient amount to use for training, and, furthermore, there are a few number of frame annotation for questions in our best knowledge, in both of English and Korean. Thus our system is built by using existing NLP tools without training process.

Coverage for questions

In this paper, we choose the SP approach to interpret questions. To according with this, the system should deal with the various type of questions and analyse the requirements of the question interpretation task in KBQA.

Use standardized format

The system will be used for question interpretation module to generate machine readable query, SPARQL. To publish our system as an open-source, all of results is in JSON and RDF format for the convenience for the other users who want to use it for their KBQA system.

3.2 Q-frame and Q-FE Identification

In this section, the process, Q-frame/Q-FE identification is described.

We figure out that there are three type of questions.

Table 1 The Rules for Q-frame and Q-FE Identification based on the Question Type

Question Pattern	Question Type	Dependency of Q-frame	Root Node
What is the naval warfare … ?	1	NP_SBJ, dist=1	VNP
What the naval warfare … ?	1	NP_SBJ, dist=1	NP
Is the naval warfare … ?	2	NP_SBJ, dist=0	NP_SBJ
The naval warfare … ?	2	NP, 0	NP
Describe about the naval warfare … .	3	NP_OBJ, dist=0	VP

The tag `NP_SBJ` is for the noun phrase which roles as a subject in a sentence, and `NP_OBJ` roles as an object. The tag `VP` is for verb phrase, and `VNP` is for the verb phrase as the copula.

The type 1 is a typical factoid question, for instance, "What was the naval warfare…?". In the type 1, the question word, Q-FE, is represented within interrogative pronouns. The type 2 is a question without the interrogative pronouns. This case is well-shown in many Korean questions, such as "The naval warfare commanded by Admiral Yi Sun-sin?". The type 3 is a imperative sentence, for example, "Describe about the naval warfare which…". To cover three type of questions, our system is built by using the rules that we designed in Table 1. For our example question, "What is the naval warfare…?", our system finds the head node in the dependency structure and figure out its phrase tag, `NP`, and find its child nodes (dist=1) and its phrase tag, `NP_SBJ`. And then our system figures out the word "naval warfare" as a target word that evokes Q-frame, `frame:Event`. And then the system identifies Q-FE based on its question type. If the type is 2 or 3, the system makes a virtual node for Q-FE, and if the type is 1, the root node is considered as Q-FE. Figure 2 shows the result for our example question.

In Figure 2, the system identifies the word "the naval warfare" as a target of Q-frame, and the word "What" as Q-FE by using the rules. And then each word is assigned to frames by using the mapping table which consists of word-frame pair based on the 6,820 lexical units in Korean FrameNet[4]. In our example, the word "the naval warfare" is assigned to `frame:Event`, so that the expected answer type is considered as an Event.

---

[3] https://framenet.icsi.berkeley.edu/fndrupal/
[4] http://framenet.kaist.ac.kr

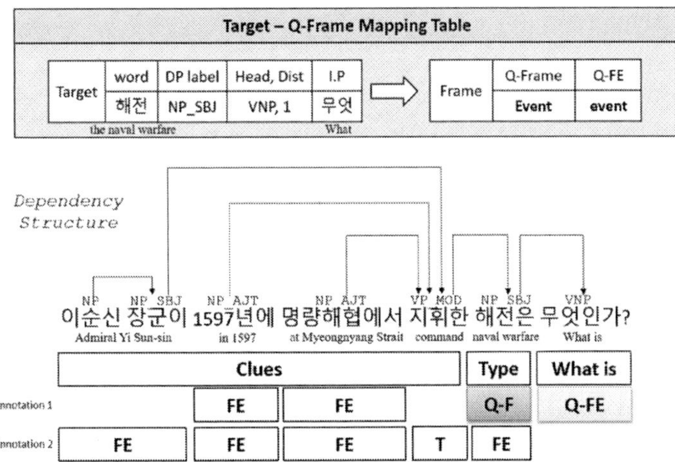

Figure 2 Q-frame and Q-FE Identification and Target-frame Mapping using Dependency

3.3   Sub-frame Identification

The purpose of Sub-frame is to include the clues of questions in query, for example, <?x, p, o> format triple patterns in SPARQL query, for information such as "commanded by Admiral Yi Sun-sin", "at Myeongyang Strait", and "in 1597" in our example question. To generate these triple patterns, the system uses the predicate-arguments structure based on the frames in a question. In this paper, we use the existing Korean SRL tool (Lim *et al.*, 2014) to analyse predicate-arguments structure.

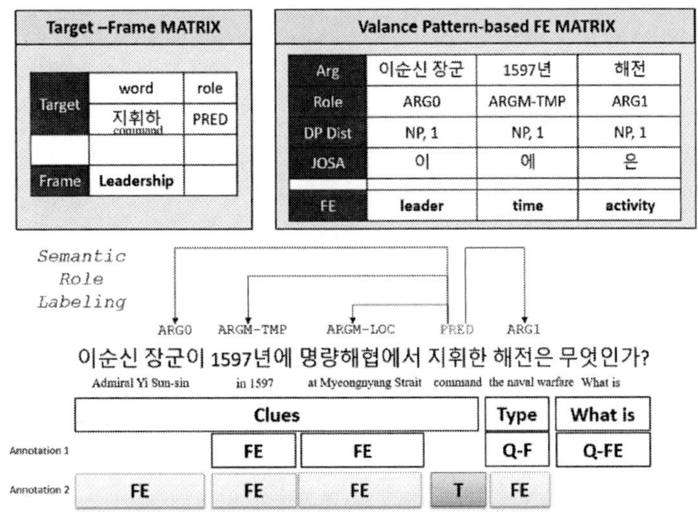

Figure 3 Sub-frame Identification using SRL

SRL tool identifies the target word of Sub-frame by using an identified predicate of sentence. Each FEs are identified by using arguments that identified by SRL also. And then each target word is assigned to the frames by using the mapping table which is used in the Q-frame identification process. The valence pattern is a grammatical condition of each FE. In Figure 3, the argument "Admiral Yi Sun-sin" is assigned to the FE tag `fe:leader` by combining the condition of josa and SRL tag.

However, sometimes SRL tool does not figure out the predicate-arguments structure for some questions, and several arguments are not identified also in some cases. Especially, the node Q-FE in QAF is used to connect each predicate-arguments graph, so that Q-FE should be identified. We developed several post-processing modules to handle these problems.

3.4 Post-processing

For the sentence without predicates

The PropBank-style SRL tools does not figure out the predicate-arguments structure for sentences without verbs. However, in the question "Who is the member of the Singanhoe?", the word "member" implicits that the expected answer type is a PERSON, and the phrase "the member of the Singanhoe" includes the clues to answer the question. Thus, even though there are no predicate-arguments structure in the question, information of question should be represented in the query. Our system outputs this results as a clue of the question; <Member, description, Member of the Singanhoe>

Handling undetected arguments

The target words of Q-frame connect each frame graph in QAF. However, in some case, the target word of Q-frame is not identified in the other frame graphs as an argument. Thus, if a predicate-arguments graph failed to identify the target words as an argument, our system adds it as an argument for all of predicate-arguments graph which does not include it.

Connect each predicate-arguments graph

In SRL results, each identified predicate-arguments graph is in each independent annotation layer. Our system connects each graphs by matching the spans of each argument.

Phrase chunking

Existing Korean SLR tools identify only a last token (called *eojeol* in Korean) of a noun phrase as an argument. The phrase chunking module is developed for our system to identify noun phrases as arguments in predicate-arguments graphs. Conjunctive noun phrases are considered as arguments of the predicate, and *josa* (particles in Korean) is dropped out of arguments.

3.5 QAF result

As a result of our system, QAF is generated from a question based on RDF format. For our example question, "What was the naval warfare commanded by Admiral Yi Sun-sin at Myeongyang Strait in 1597?", our system outputs;

```
frdf-event:해전#1                                      (the naval warfare)
        rdf:type      frame:Event           ;
        fe:name       ?answer               ;

frdf-event:지휘하#1                                     (command)
        fe:leader     "이순신 장군"          ;          (Admiral Yi Sun-sin)
        fe:time       "1597 년"              ;          (1597)
        fe:place      "명량해협"             ;          (Myeongyang Strait)
        fe:activity   frdf-event:해전#1      .          (the naval warfare)
```

The target words, "the naval warfare" and "command", are given URIs (Uniform Resource Identifiers) and role as a subject in triples, and the arguments role as an object in triples. The FE tags is used as properties. QAF does not represents binary relations, like DBpedia, but represents events and its elements in the RDF format by using the method that n-ary relation with creating a individual (in our example, frdf:event) to role as a subject and generating links to all arguments with the FE tags which role as properties. This event-centric representation would cover the complex information in questions based on the frame structure.

4　Evaluation and Discussion

4.1　Frame Identification

The evaluation is performed on the NLQ50[5] data in OKBQA. We use 45 questions excepting O/X questions and description question as our test data.

For 45 questions, our system identifies all target words of Q-frame for every question, and 51 target words of Sub-frames also. 58 frames are assigned for 96 target words, and all of frames are correctly assigned by manual evaluation. And our system identifies 36 FEs of Sub-frames. By manual evaluation, Sub-frame identification task is evaluated as Table 2.

Table 2 Evaluation of Frame Identification

Task	Precision	Recall	F1
Frame Identification	1.0	0.6041	0.7531
FE Identification	0.90	0.73	0.8137

4.2　Discussion

Frame identification

Our system uses the lexical units of Korean FrameNet to assign the frames to target words. However, the coverage of the lexical units is about 60%, so that it is required to increase the overall performance. As future work, we plan to develop the frame identification module based on the word embedding approach (Hermann *et al.*, 2014) to increase the coverage.

For the multiple questions

In the scope of this paper, our system deals with only a single sentence question. Although it performs well, but it is required to handle multiple sentence questions, such as a complex sentence, O/X questions, and multiple choice questions. Especially we focus on the multiple sentence question as the future work.

Ontology mapping

QAF is a format based on the frames to represent information of questions in structured format with assuming that there is the imaginary KB. To develop a question interpretation system for existing KBs, it is required to map QAF with SPARQL underlying its ontological schemas.

5　Conclusion

In this paper we designed a format, QAF, to represent complex information of questions in the event-centric RDF format. The KB-dependent approach extracts only binary relations from questions, and it involves the limitation of coverage of question interpretation because of the incompleteness of KB. And the schemas in KBs does not cover the all of the lexical meaning in questions also. For this reason, we propose the semantic parsing approach based on the frame semantics to analyse complex information in questions. And then we developed the system which translates Korean questions into QAF. Handling multiple sentence questions and mapping QAF to existing KBs are remains as the future works.

Acknowledgments

This work was supported by Institute for Information & communications Technology Promotion(IITP) grant funded by the Korea government(MSIP)
(No. R0101-16-0054, WiseKB: Big data based self-evolving knowledge base and reasoning platform)

This work was supported by the Bio & Medical Technology Development Program of the NRF funded by the Korean government, MSIP(2015M3A9A7029735)

---

[5] http://3.okbqa.org/development/resources

Reference

Sören Auer, Christian Bizer, Georgi Kobilarov, Jens Lehmann, Richard Cyganiak. 2007. Dbpedia: A nucleus for a web of open data. In *The semantic web*. Springer Berlin Heidelberg, 722-735.

Collin F. Baker, Charles J. Fillmore, John B. Lowe. 1998. The berkeley framenet project. In *Proceedings of the 36th Annual Meeting of the Association for Computational Linguistics and 17th International Conference on Computational Linguistics-Volume 1* (pp. 86-90). Association for Computational Linguistics.

Jonathan Berant, Percy Liang. 2014. Semantic Parsing via Paraphrasing. In *ACL* (1) (pp. 1415-1425).

Kurt Bollacker, Coling Evans, Praveen Paritosh, Tim Sturge, and Jamie Taylor. 2008. Freebase: a collaboratively created graph database for structuring human knowledge. In *Proceedings of the 2008 ACM SIGMOD international conference on Management of data*. ACM.

Dipanjan Das, Nathan Schneider, Desai Chen, Noah A. Smith. 2010. SEMAFOR 1.0: A probabilistic frame-semantic parser. *Language Technologies Institute, School of Computer Science, Carnegie Mellon University*.

Younggyun Hahm, Youngsik Kim, Yousung Won, Jongsung Woo, Jiwoo Seo, Jiseong Kim, Seongbae Park, Dosam Hwang, Key-Sun Choi. 2014. Toward Matching the Relation Instantiation from DBpedia Ontology to Wikipedia Text: Fusing FrameNet to Korean, In *Proceedings of iSemantics 2014*.

Karl Moritz Hermann, Dipanjan Das, Jason Weston, Kuzman Ganchev. 2014. zSemantic frame identification with distributed word representations. In *ACL*.

Johannes Hoffart, Fabian M Suchanek, Klaus Berberich, Gerhard Weikum. 2013. YAGO2: A spatially and temporally enhanced knowledge base from Wikipedia. *Artificial Intelligence*, 194, 28-61.

Soojong Lim, Changki Lee, Pum-Mo Ryu, Hyunki Kim, Sangkyu Park, Dongyul Ra. 2014. A Domain Adaptation Technique for Semantic Role Labeling with Structural Learning. In *ETRI Journal* vol. 36, no. 3, June. 2014, pp. 429-438.

Mike Mintz, Steven Bills, Rion Snow, Dan Jurafsky. 2009, A. Distant supervision for relation extraction without labeled data. In *Proceedings of the Joint Conference of the 47th Annual Meeting of the ACL and the 4th International Joint Conference on Natural Language Processing of the AFNLP*: Volume 2-Volume 2 (pp. 1003-1011). Association for Computational Linguistics.

Sangha Nam, Younggyun Hahm, Sejin Nam, Key-Sun Choi. 2015. SRDF: Korean Open Information Extraction using Singleton Property. In *Proceedings of International Semantic Web Conference, ISWC, Posters & Demonstrations Track*.

Jungyeul Park, Sejin Nam, Youngsik Kim, Younggyun Hahm, Dosam Hwang, Key-Sun Choi, 2014. Frame Semantic Web: A Case Study for Korean, In *Proceedings of International Semantic Web Conference*, ISWC.

Jacobo Rouces, Gerard de Melo, Katja Hose. 2015. FrameBase: representing n-ary relations using semantic frames. In *European Semantic Web Conference* (pp. 505-521). Springer International Publishing.

Christina Unger, Lorenz Bühmann, Jens Lehmann, Axel-Cyrille Ngonga Ngomo, Daniel Gerber, Philipp Cimiano. 2012. Template-based question answering over RDF data. In *Proceedings of the 21st international conference on World Wide Web* (pp. 639-648). ACM.

Piek Vossen, German Rigau, Luciano Serafini, Pim Stouten, Francis Irving, Willem Van Hage. 2014. NewsReader: recording history from daily news streams. In *LREC* (pp. 2000-2007).

Kun Xu, Sheng Zhang, Yansong Feng, and Dongyan Zhao. 2014. Answering Natural Language Questions via Phrasal Semantic Parsing. In *Natural Language Processing and Chinese Computing* (pp. 333-344). Springer Berlin Heidelberg.

Xuchen Yao, Jonathan Berant, Benjamin Van Durme. 2014. Freebase QA: Information Extraction or Semantic Parsing?. In *ACL* 2014, 82. (a)

Xuchen Yao, Benjamin Van Durme. 2014. Information Extraction over Structured Data: Question Answering with Freebase. In *ACL* (1) (pp. 956-966). (b)

Answering Yes-No Questions by Penalty Scoring in History Subjects of University Entrance Examinations

Yoshinobu Kano

Faculty of Informatics, Shizuoka University, Japan

`kano@inf.shizuoka.ac.jp`

Abstract

Answering yes–no questions is more difficult than simply retrieving ranked search results. To answer yes–no questions, especially when the correct answer is no, one must find an objectionable keyword that makes the question's answer no. Existing systems, such as factoid-based ones, cannot answer yes–no questions very well because of insufficient handling of such objectionable keywords. We suggest an algorithm that answers yes–no questions by assigning an importance to objectionable keywords. Concretely speaking, we suggest a penalized scoring method that finds and makes lower score for parts of documents that include such objectionable keywords. We check a keyword distribution for each part of a document such as a paragraph, calculating the keyword density as a basic score. Then we use an objectionable keyword penalty when a keyword does not appear in a target part but appears in other parts of the document. Our algorithm is robust for open domain problems because it requires no machine learning. We achieved 4.45 point better results in F1 scores than the best score of the NTCIR-10 RITE2 shared task, also obtained the best score in 2014 mock university examination challenge of the Todai Robot project.

1 Introduction

Although its importance has long been recognized (Hirschberg, 1984; Green et al., 1994), yes–no question answering (QA) has not been studied well compared to other types of QA such as factoid-style QA (Ravichandran et al., 2002; Bian et al., 2008) and non-factoid complex QA (Kelly et al., 2007), including definition QA (Cui et al., 2005; Xu et al., 2003).

As described herein, we propose an approach to answer yes–no questions. Our main claim is that it is necessary to handle *objectionable* keywords in *no* questions that are insufficiently considered in previous studies. We claim that this is the greatest difference in yes–no QA from other QA tasks. We suggest a penalized scoring method that finds and makes lower scores for objectionable keywords. This method can classify yes–no answers more sharply, overcoming the white noise effects described below.

In spite of the apparent simplicity that a yes–no question is a binary decision, it is not easy to answer. One might consider the following yes–no question.

(1) Is it dangerous to use an acidic cleaner with *enzyme* bleach?

A slightly different question can be posed by replacing *enzyme* with *chlorine*.

(2) Is it dangerous to use an acidic cleaner with *chlorine* bleach?

Example (1) includes the keywords *dangerous, acidic cleaner*, and *enzyme bleach*, while (2) includes *chlorine bleach* instead of *enzyme bleach*. Correct answers are *no* for (1) and *yes* for (2).

The standard means of answering yes–no questions would be to ask a search engine using keywords extracted as shown above. A search engine can return ranked results with confidence values. Comparing the topmost confidence values of yes and no questions, we can determine yes or no. However, standard search engines do not expect an objectionable keyword, *enzyme bleach* in (1). Therefore, they do not make a sufficient difference between (1) and (2), do not directly function for yes–no questions.

Yes–no QA can also be regarded as an application of factoid-style QA systems. In fact, (2) can be converted into the following.

(3) *What* is dangerous to use an acidic cleaner with?

Proceedings of the Open Knowledge Base and Question Answering (OKBQA) Workshop,
pages 91–96, Osaka, Japan, December 11 2016.

By replacing *chlorine bleach* with *What*, a factoid-style QA system (Mitamura et al., 2010) can provide an answer to question (3) such as *chlorine bleach*. By comparing the answer with the original question's keyword such as *chlorine bleach* in (2), *yes* or *no* can be assigned for each question (Prager et al., 2006). However, this conversion process includes a large part of the entire solution process as described below. The next example adds *in a washing machine* to (2), thereby producing the following question.

(4) Is it dangerous to use an acidic cleaner with chlorine bleach *in a washing machine*?

This addition does not affect the yes–no answer. When converting this question into a factoid-style question, which keyword to replace is a critical and difficult issue (Kanayama et al., 2012; Ishioroshi et al., 2014). The best system (Kobayashi et al., 2016) in the World History of the Todai Robot project's mock exam challenge combined different methods that make effective features unclear. These previous works leave some issues unresolved, what is the key feature to answer yes-no questions.

In either case, finding an objectionable keyword is the missing issue. Ideally speaking, all the keywords would co-occur in an evidence description of the knowledge source if the answer is *yes*. Unfortunately, keyword extraction is not perfect because it is extremely difficult to determine an unrelated keyword such as *washing machine*. Distribution of such an unrelated keyword has no relation to the co-occurrence of relevant and objectionable keywords. Consequently, it makes a sort of white noise in scoring. This effect produces a score difference between relevant and objectionable keywords vague. Standard frequency-based algorithms will not answer yes–no questions adequately.

Recognition of Textual Entailment (RTE) is another related task to the yes–no QA. RTE has recently been studied intensively, including shared tasks such as RTE tasks of PASCAL (Dagan et al., 2006; Giampiccolo et al., 2007), SemEval-2012 Cross-lingual Textual Entailment (CLTE) (Negri et al., 2012), and NTCIR RITE tasks (Kanayama et al., 2012). NTCIR-9 RITE (Shima et al., 2011) and NTCIR-10 RITE2's Exam Search tasks (Watanabe et al., 2013) required participants to find an evidence in source documents and to answer a given proposition according to yes or no. In this most realistic setting, no candidate sentence is given explicitly. One can consider the following, which is converted from question (1) of an interrogative form into an affirmative form.

(5) *It is* dangerous to use an acidic cleaner with enzyme bleach.

Judging entailment of (5) in a given source document is equivalent to answering yes–no question (1). Therefore, this style of RTEs can also be regarded as yes–no questions.

We describe details of our proposed method and implementation (Section 2), experiments and results (Section 3), discussion with potential future works (Section 4), and conclude the paper (Section 5).

2 Method and Implementation

Roughly speaking, our system performs (a) keyword extraction from the input, (b) keyword weighting of the input, and (c) source document search and scoring. Figure 1 shows our system architecture conceptually.

2.1 Keyword Extraction

We applied the same keyword extraction method both for the question text and the knowledge source text.

We performed an exact match in the given text for each page title of Wikipedia entries, and used matched titles as keywords. When exact match keywords overlap, we used only the longest match keyword, discarding shorter ones. Some page titles, such as single-letter words, were discarded manually to avoid illegal named entity matching. We regarded all page titles of Wikipedia's redirect pages as synonyms, i.e. identical words.

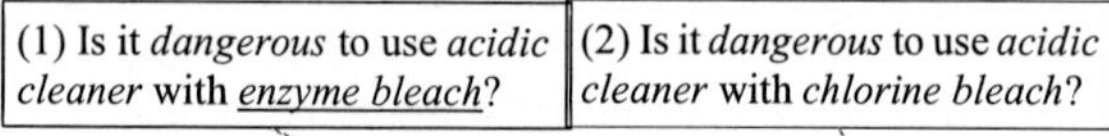

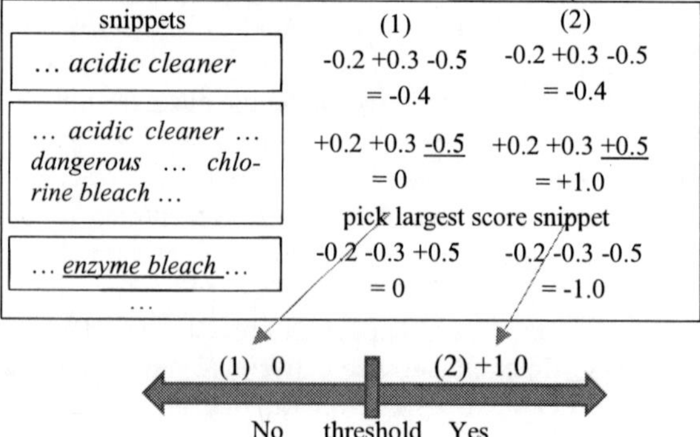

Figure 1. Conceptual figure of our system architecture.

Table 1. NTCIR-10 RITE2 Exam Search Results

| source | total # | proposed model | | | | | | baseline textbook | best in RITE2 |
| | | Textbook | | | wikipedia | | | | |
snippet		sec	sub	p	sec	sub	p	p	p
Y-F1		52.08	55.19	56.30	16.59	16.38	12.67	52.05	41.76
Y-Precision	173	47.39	52.33	60.69	10.98	32.20	29.17	49.48	57.00
Y-Recall		57.80	58.38	52.50	33.93	10.98	8.09	54.91	32.95
N-F1		64.06	69.06	68.83	71.36	70.78	71.41	67.04	74.48
N-Precision	275	69.20	71.76	72.58	60.71	60.41	60.25	69.53	66.67
N-Recall		59.64	66.55	65.45	86.55	85.45	87.64	64.73	84.36
Macro F1	448	58.07	62.12	**62.57**	43.98	43.58	42.04	59.55	58.12

Evaluation results in correct answer ratio of RITE2 official evaluation metric (b=3.2). source is knowledge source document. snippet is snippet unit: section (sec), subsection (sub), paragraph (p). Y/N-xx is correct answer yes/no.

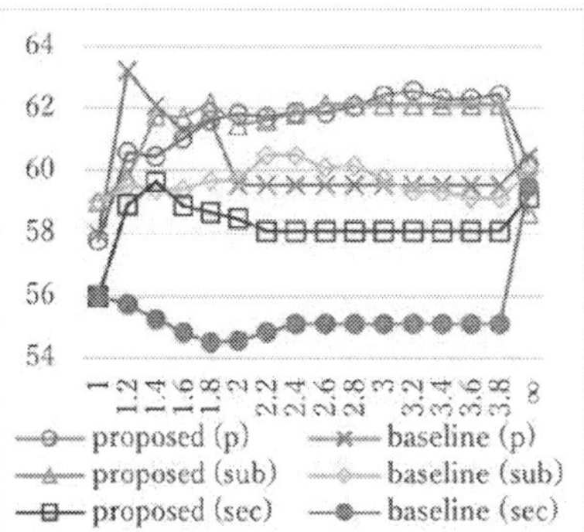

Figure 2. F1 scores w.r.t bias parameters.

2.2 Keyword Weighting

We assign a weight for each keyword that represents the importance of that keyword. Let c_i be the frequency of i-th distinct keyword in given knowledge source document. Then the weight of the i-th keyword is the following.

$$w_i = 1/(c_i z) + b$$

In this equation, $z = \sum_i 1/c_i$ is a normalizing constant, where i is defined over the distinct keywords in the input. Also, b is a constant bias term that is optimized experimentally. A larger value of b decreases the effect of weight difference between keywords.

2.3 Document Search and Scoring

We assume that a relevant part of documents densely contains relevant keywords in a given question. This assumption is similar to most other existing methods.

We divide the source document data into snippets such as paragraphs. Snippets are manually predefined in our experiment knowledge source. We search for a snippet that has the highest score with respect to the input keyword set K.

When a keyword such as *enzymatic bleaching* does not appear in a target snippet of the document, but appears in another snippet of the document, then we regard that keyword as objectionable with respect to the target snippet of the document and assign a lower score to the target snippet. This penalty enables us to construct a high-precision QA system using simple techniques. Let R be the keyword set extracted from a snippet. Then the score of R is

$$s_R = \sum_{l \in R \cap K} w_l - \sum_{m \in K - R} w_m$$

The first term of this expression means that the basic score of the snippet is the sum of the weights of the input keywords included in the snippet. The second term is a penalty term that subtracts the sum of the weights of the input keywords that are not included in the snippet, but included in another snippet. If a given choice is correct, then keywords in the choice should be included densely in a specific snippet of the source document. If a given choice is wrong, then its keywords should be scattered across snippets. The equation above penalizes such a scattered keyword distribution. Finally, we regard the maximum s_R among all snippets as the confidence score of the corresponding input. Yes–no is decided by comparison of the score with a threshold value, an average confidence score over a given dataset in our case.

We do not consider negations because it is rare for questions and source documents to describe events in a negative form.

3 Experiments and Results

The RITE2 Exam Search subtask was designed originally as an RTE task in which participants return true or false for a given proposition by referring to textual knowledge, such as Wikipedia and textbooks, with no candidate sentence in the knowledge source specified. The RITE2 dataset was developed from past Japanese National Center Test questions for the University Admissions (Center Test). The questions were presented originally in a multiple-choice style of questions. Because each choice corresponds to true or false, each choice can be regarded as a single yes–no question. Participant systems are asked to return yes or no with a confidence value for each question.

The dataset consists of a development set of 528 yes–no questions and a test set of 448 yes–no questions. All of our evaluation results are on the test set using the RITE2 official evaluation tool. Since our system requires no machine learning, we did not use the development set.

We used knowledge sources of two types: high school textbooks and Wikipedia. Both are written in Japanese. We tried three types of snippets: section, subsection, paragraph, larger to smaller in this order. Boundaries of these snippets are explicitly marked in textbooks by the textbook authors.

Wikipedia has its own document structures. For comparison with textbooks, we regarded a Wikipedia page as a section, sections in a page as subsections, and paragraphs as paragraphs. For efficiency, we used Wikipedia pages for which titles detected in the test datasets. This arrangement does not affect results because our keyword extraction is performed using the very same set of Wikipedia titles.

Table 1 shows results of *our proposed model, our baseline*, and the *best of RITE2* participant. The *source* row shows which knowledge source was used: either *textbook* or *Wikipedia*. The *snippet* row shows the snippet unit: *section, subsection,* or *paragraph*. Our baseline model is equivalent to the suggested model, except for dropping the penalty term, to check the effect of the penalty term. The baseline model becomes $s_R = \sum_{l \in R \cap K} w_l$.

In the Macro F1 score, which was the primary metric in RITE2 balancing yes and no answers, our best system (knowledge source is *textbook* and snippet is *paragraph*) performed 5.45 points better than the best result in RITE2. Our best system performed 3.02 points better than our *baseline,* showing the effect of a penalty. Among the snippet units in our suggested method, *paragraph* using *textbook* obtained the best score overall. Results using *textbook* were better than those using *Wikipedia*. *Wikipedia* results do not show a clear difference irrespective of the snippet units.

Figure 2 shows a graph of the Macro F1 score with respect to the bias term b, with values of 1.0–3.8. The notation of ∞ is assigned when no weight is used. Comparison of pairs of *proposed* and *baseline* for each snippet shows that the *baseline* is almost always lower than *proposed*, i.e. the penalty term is effective. Table 1 corresponds to a bias value of $b = 3.2$.

4 Discussion

The result shows that our penalty scoring is effective in yes-no question answering.

Although we observed that keyword extraction was successful, keyword selection was difficult. A keyword that has no relation with the answer to the question could decrease the performance, even if our method is used.

The document structure granularity is another issue. Depending on a given question, a corresponding part of knowledge source differs. Its evidence might be described in a single sentence, or may be written using several sentences scattered across subsections. Our results imply that *paragraphs* are approximately the average size of the snippet per evidence description because *paragraphs* obtained the best score.

While result scores obtained using textbooks show a clear decreasing tendency when changing the snippet unit from smaller to larger, result scores obtained using Wikipedia are not clear. Write styles are different between textbooks' professional writers and Wikipedia's numerous anonymous writers. These differences are expected to produce various granularities in which part the evidence of a question we search for is described, producing the incoherent results. However, our results suggest that Wikipedia is still useful because of the word-based links, absorbing fluctuation of description and synonym variations.

A more difficult problem is the treatment of verbs. Noun synonyms can be covered well by the Wikipedia redirect relations and other existing dictionaries. However, finding relations between a pair of verbs is difficult. For example, to *suppress* someone and to *preserve* someone could be exclusive relations depending on their context; it would be difficult to produce such an exclusive word pair dictionary not just because it might depend on the context but also because the potential pairs are numerous.

While there is a couple of future work above, an advantage of our method is that no training is necessary when constructing the QA system. Another advantage is that we do not use any category of named entities. For these reasons, our system is domain-independent and robust for open-domain problems.

Our proposed method above is independent of any specific language. We can simply translate extracted keywords into the source document to perform cross-lingual searching if the given question is in a language (e.g. English) but not the same as a source document language (e.g. Japanese).

5   Conclusion and Future Work

We presented our method, which assigns importance to the objectionable keywords to answer yes–no questions accurately. We conducted experiments using the NTCIR-10 RITE2 shared task and others for comparison with previous studies. Results show that our system is a state-of-the-art system on the RITE2 task by 4.45 points better than the previous best system. The same system obtained the best score in World History of the mock examination challenge 2014 of the Todai Robot project. These results show that our penalty scoring is an effective feature to solve yes-no question answering.

Future work includes a better keyword selection depending on the context. A better scoring way using more precise document structure, and optimizing the yes–no threshold can also improve the results.

Reference

Bian, J., Liu, Y., Agichtein, E. and Zha, H. (2008). Finding the Right Facts in the Crowd: Factoid Question Answering over Social Media. *Proceedings of the 17th International Conference on World Wide Web*, WWW '08 (pp. 467–476). inproceedings, New York, NY, USA: ACM. doi:10.1145/1367497.1367561

Cui, H., Kan, M.-Y. and Chua, T.-S. (2005). Generic Soft Pattern Models for Definitional Question Answering. *Proceedings of the 28th Annual International ACM SIGIR Conference on Research and Development in Information Retrieval*, SIGIR '05 (pp. 384–391). inproceedings, New York, NY, USA: ACM. doi:10.1145/1076034.1076101

Dagan, I., Glickman, O. and Magnini, B. (2006). The PASCAL Recognising Textual Entailment Challenge. *Proceedings of the First International Conference on Machine Learning Challenges: Evaluating Predictive Uncertainty Visual Object Classification, and Recognizing Textual Entailment*, MLCW'05 (pp. 177–190). inproceedings, Berlin, Heidelberg: Springer-Verlag. doi:10.1007/11736790_9

Giampiccolo, D., Magnini, B., Dagan, I. and Dolan, B. (2007). The Third PASCAL Recognizing Textual Entailment Challenge. *Proceedings of the ACL-PASCAL Workshop on Textual Entailment and Paraphrasing*, RTE '07 (pp. 1–9). inproceedings, Stroudsburg, PA, USA: Association for Computational Linguistics. Retrieved from http://dl.acm.org/citation.cfm?id=1654536.1654538

Green, N. and Carberry, S. (1994). Generating Indirect Answers to Yes-No Questions. *Proceedings of the Seventh International Workshop on Natural Language Generation*, INLG '94 (pp. 189–198). inproceedings, Stroudsburg, PA, USA: Association for Computational Linguistics. Retrieved from http://dl.acm.org/citation.cfm?id=1641417.1641439

Hirschberg, J. (1984). Toward a Redefinition of Yes/No Questions. *Proceedings of the 10th International Conference on Computational Linguistics and 22Nd Annual Meeting on Association for Computational Linguistics*, ACL '84 (pp. 48–51). inproceedings, Stroudsburg, PA, USA: Association for Computational Linguistics. doi:10.3115/980491.980503

Ishioroshi, M., Kano, Y. and Kando, N. (2014). A multiple-choice problem solver using question-answering system. *SIG Technical Reports, IPSJ-NL*.

Kanayama, H., Miyao, Y. and Prager, J. (2012). Answering Yes/No Questions via Question Inversion. *the 24th International Conference on Computational Linguistics (COLING 2012)* (pp. 1377–1391). Mumbai, India.

Kelly, D. and Lin, J. (2007). Overview of the TREC 2006 ciQA Task. *SIGIR Forum*, *41*(1), 107–116. article, New York, NY, USA: ACM. doi:10.1145/1273221.1273231

Kobayashi, M., Miyashita, H., Ishii, A. and Hoshino, C. (2016). NUL System at QA Lab-2 Task. *NTCIR-12 workshop* (pp. 413–420). Tokyo, Japan.

Mitamura, T., Shima, H., Sakai, T., Kando, N., Mori, T., Takeda, K., Lin, C.-Y., Song, R., Lin, C.-J., et al. (2010). Overview of the NTCIR-8 ACLIA Tasks: Advanced Cross-Lingual Information Access. *NTCIR-8 Workshop*.

Negri, M., Marchetti, A., Mehdad, Y., Bentivogli, L. and Giampiccolo, D. (2012). Semeval-2012 Task 8: Cross-lingual Textual Entailment for Content Synchronization. *Proceedings of the First Joint Conference on Lexical and Computational Semantics - Volume 1: Proceedings of the Main Conference and the Shared*

Task, and Volume 2: Proceedings of the Sixth International Workshop on Semantic Evaluation, SemEval '12 (pp. 399–407). inproceedings, Stroudsburg, PA, USA: Association for Computational Linguistics. Retrieved from http://dl.acm.org/citation.cfm?id=2387636.2387700

Prager, J., Duboue, P. and Chu-Carroll, J. (2006). Improving QA Accuracy by Question Inversion. *Proceedings of the 21st International Conference on Computational Linguistics and the 44th Annual Meeting of the Association for Computational Linguistics*, ACL-44 (pp. 1073–1080). inproceedings, Stroudsburg, PA, USA: Association for Computational Linguistics. doi:10.3115/1220175.1220310

Ravichandran, D. and Hovy, E. (2002). Learning Surface Text Patterns for a Question Answering System. *Proceedings of the 40th Annual Meeting on Association for Computational Linguistics*, ACL '02 (pp. 41–47). inproceedings, Stroudsburg, PA, USA: Association for Computational Linguistics. doi:10.3115/1073083.1073092

Shima, H., Kanayama, H., Lee, C., Lin, C., Mitamura, T., Miyao, Y., Shi, S. and Takeda, K. (2011). Overview of NTCIR-9 RITE: Recognizing Inference in TExt. *NTCIR-9 Workshop* (pp. 291–301). inproceedings, .

Watanabe, Y., Miyao, Y., Mizuno, J., Shibata, T., Kanayama, H., Lee, C.-W., Lin, C.-J., Shi, S., Mitamura, T., et al. (2013). Overview of the Recognizing Inference in Text (RITE-2) at NTCIR-10. *the NTCIR-10 Workshop* (pp. 385–404). Tokyo, Japan.

Xu, J., Licuanan, A. and Weischedel, R. M. (2003). TREC 2003 QA at BBN: Answering Definitional Questions. *TREC* (pp. 98–106). inproceedings, .

Dedicated Workflow Management for OKBQA Framework

Jiseong Kim, GyuHyeon Choi, Key-Sun Choi
Machine Reading Laboratory
Semantic Web Research Center
Department of Computer Science
KAIST, Daejeon, Korea
`{jiseong, wianyll, kschoi}@kaist.ac.kr`

Abstract

Nowadays, a question answering (QA) system is used in various areas such a quiz show, personal assistant, home device, and so on. The OKBQA framework supports developing a QA system in an intuitive and collaborative ways. To support collaborative development, the framework should be equipped with some functions, e.g., flexible system configuration, debugging supports, intuitive user interface, and so on while considering different developing groups of different domains. This paper presents OKBQA controller, a dedicated workflow manager for OKBQA framework, to boost collaborative development of a QA system.

1 Introduction

Recently, a QA system have been on the rise being applied to diverse domains, e.g., quiz show (IBM Watson), personal assistant (Apple Siri, Microsoft Cortana), home device (Amazon Echo), and so on.

To make a QA system, the OKBQA framework focuses on constructing an OKBQA pipeline-based QA system. The OKBQA pipeline is based on the state-of-the-art researches such as template generation (Unger et al., 2012), disambiguation (Usbeck et al., 2014), query generation (Kim and Cohen, 2014), and so on, which is depicted in Figure 1.

The main goal of the OKBQA framework is to support **collaborative development** of an OKBQA pipeline-based QA system, To support the collaborative development, the framework should be equipped with key functions:

- **Pipeline construction based on OKBQA specification** As modules of the OKBQA pipeline are developed by different groups of different domains, I/O specification is crucial to integrate modules developed independently into an integrated whole system. The OKBQA specification specifies that an I/O format of OKBQA module should be a JSON format and their interface should be implemented as a REST API. That is, the (OKBQA) framework should be capable of linking modules of JSON-formatted I/O with a RESTful service. By compliance with the OKBQA specification, modules developed by a different groups can be integrated into one QA system.

- **Flexible pipeline configuration** By open collaboration, an QA system can be constructed by modules developed by different developers. To support a developer who wants to construct his QA system by reusing some modules developed by other developers, the framework should be equipped with the function of configuring which modules will compose his QA system.

- **Debugging supports** As different users can develop a module of a QA system independently, some modules can cause a crash of an entire system by diverse errors. To support developers chasing a cause of errors, the framework should be capable of showing exceptional information about which module is crashed, the input causing the crash, and the reason why the module is crashed.

- **Intuitive user interface** To support developers of diverse domains, the framework should provide an intuitive and common user interface that can lower the entry barrier of QA system development.

Proceedings of the Open Knowledge Base and Question Answering (OKBQA) Workshop,
pages 97–101, Osaka, Japan, December 11 2016.

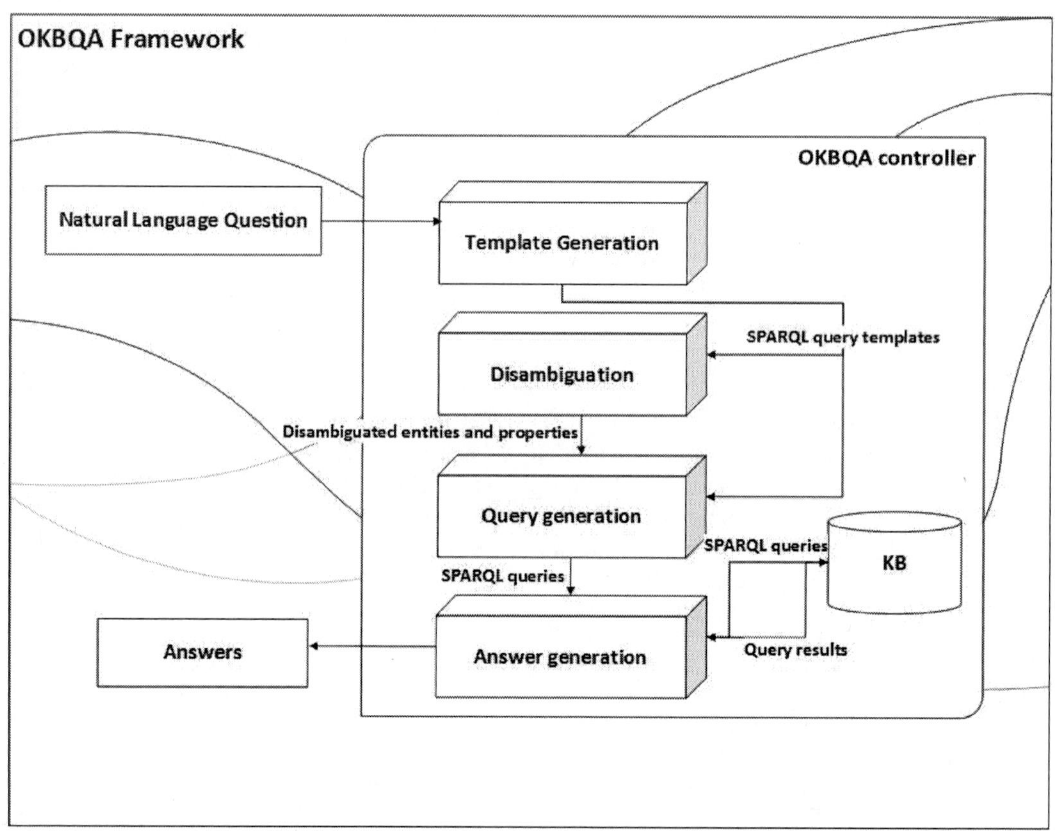

Figure 1: Workflow of an OKBQA pipeline

The above-mentioned functions are traditionally dealt by a workflow manager, which is a kind of a module for linking other modules to construct an integrated system. In this paper, we present a dedicated workflow manager for the OKBQA framework, so-called **OKBQA controller**, to boost the collaborative development of an OKBQA pipeline-based QA system.

2   OKBQA Controller

The OKBQA controller is a dedicated workflow manager for constructing a OKBQA pipeline by linking OKBQA modules as shown in Figure 1. The controller makes a pipeline work by transferring I/O of each module sequentially. The controller realizes and provides the key functions described in Section 1, which is detailed in the following sections.

2.1   Pipeline construction based on OKBQA specification

The controller makes a pipeline work consistently with the OKBQA specification by linking RESTful modules of JSON-formatted I/O. The I/O of the controller, depicted in Figure 2, are also compliant with the OKBQA specification as other OKBQA modules; The controller's I/O have a JSON format and interface is implemented in a RESTful service. By compliance with the OKBQA specification, modules can be developed in a consistent ways w.r.t. their I/O and interface implementation, so the reusability of modules can be significantly enhanced.

2.2   Flexible pipeline configuration

To support constructing a pipeline with various structure and composition of modules and reusing modules developed by other developers, the controller supports configuring addresses and executing sequence

- **Input:**

```
{
    "string": "Which rivers flow through Seoul?",        ← Input question
    "language": "en",                                     ← Language of Input question
    "conf": {                                             ← Configuration field
        "address": {
            "ELU": ["http://143.248.135.150:2222/entity_linking"],
            "TGM": ["http://ws.okbqa.org:1555/templategeneration/templator/"],
            "DM": ["http://ws.okbqa.org:2357/agdistis/run"],
            "QGM": ["http://ws.okbqa.org:38401/queries"],
            "AGM": ["http://ws.okbqa.org:7744/agm"],
            "KB": [["http://143.248.135.20:45103/sparql", "http://en.dbpedia2015-10.kaist.ac.kr"]]
        },
        "sequence": ["ELU", "TGM", "DM", "QGM", "AGM", "KB"],   ← Execution sequence configuration
        "timelimit": 100                                        ← Execution timeout (per sec.)
    }
}
```

- **Output:**

```
{
    "logs": [                                    ← Log messages
        {
            1. module: "TGM",
            2. elapsed_time: 0.65011169204711914,    ← Processing time
            3. input: {...},
            4. output: [...]
        },
        ...
    ],
    "answers": [...]                             ← Answers of Input question
}
```

Figure 2: I/O of an OKBQA controller

of modules by the controller's input fields "address" and "sequence" as shown in Figure 2. By configuring the number and executing sequence of modules, developers can construct their own pipeline different from the original OKBQA pipeline to apply new idea and improve their own QA system further; For example, one idea is that if disambiguated results are provided to a template generation process as an input, there is a possibility that results of a template generation module could be improved.

2.3 Debugging supports

To support efficient debugging for collaborative development, the controller provides a fault alarming function through a log message that is the field "log" in controller's output as shown in Figure 2. The log message provides the information such as input, output, and processing time of each module, name of module throwing exception, a cause of exception, and so on; these information can be useful for chasing a cause of errors that are caused by not only our module, but also the others'. When a module throws an exception, the controller will stop executing a pipeline and return an exceptional message on log; e.g. Figure 3 shows an example of the message. By the message, developers can easily notice which module is problematic and what to do for fixing it. It is an essential function to easily chase and fix errors caused by modules developed by different developers.

2.4 Web-based user interface

The controller provides a Web-based user interface[1] to developers as shown in Figure 4. Through the graphical supports by the interface, developers can set a system configuration, integrate their modules with other developers' modules to construct an integrated QA system, and test constructed QA system by asking the pre-defined natural language questions in an easy and intuitive way.

2.5 Conclusion

We have presented a dedicated workflow manager for the OKBQA framework, so-called OKBQA controller. We showed that the OKBQA controller has an essential functions to develop a QA system in a

---

[1] http://ws.okbqa.org/web_interface

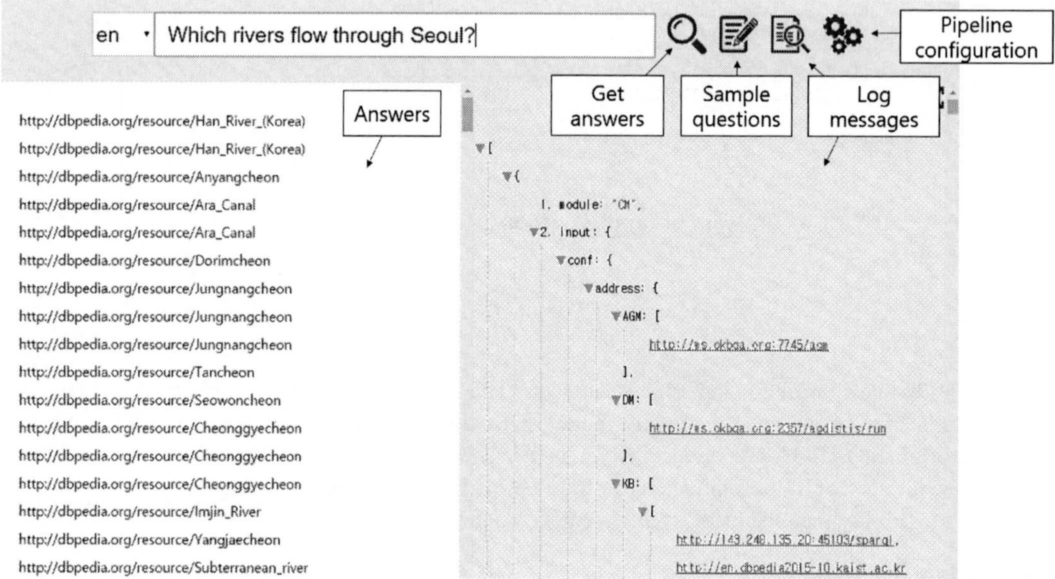

Figure 3: An example of an exceptional message

Figure 4: A Web-based user interface for an OKBQA controller

collaborative way. However, there are some points to be improved and further developed. We will keep searching needs of developers and mirroring their needs to our successive versions of the controller.

Acknowledgements

This work was supported by Institute for Information & communications Technology Promotion(IITP) grant funded by the Korea government(MSIP) (No.   R0101-16-0054, WiseKB: Big data based self-evolving knowledge base and reasoning platform).   And also this work was supported by the Bio & Medical Technology Development Program of the NRF funded by the Korean government, MSIP(2015M3A9A7029735).

References

Unger, Christina and Bühmann, Lorenz and Lehmann, Jens and Ngonga Ngomo, Axel-Cyrille and Gerber, Daniel and Cimiano, Philipp. 2012. *Template-based question answering over RDF data. Proceedings of the 21st international conference on World Wide Web* (pp. 639–648). ACM.

Usbeck, Ricardo and Ngomo, Axel-Cyrille Ngonga and Röder, Michael and Gerber, Daniel and Coelho, Sandro Athaide and Auer, Sören and Both, Andreas. 2014. *AGDISTIS-graph-based disambiguation of named entities using linked data. International Semantic Web Conference* (pp.457-471). Springer.

Kim, J. D. and Cohen, K.. 2014. *Triple pattern variation operations for flexible graph search.* *Workshop on Natural Language Interfaces for Web of Data.*

Author Index

Association for Computational Linguistics
209 N. Eighth Street
Stroudsburg, Pennsylvania 18360

ISBN 978-1-5108-3324-1